**Books are to be returned on or before
the last date below**

14 JAN 1930

22. SEP 1993

01 FEB 1995

13 JUN 1995

LIBREX —

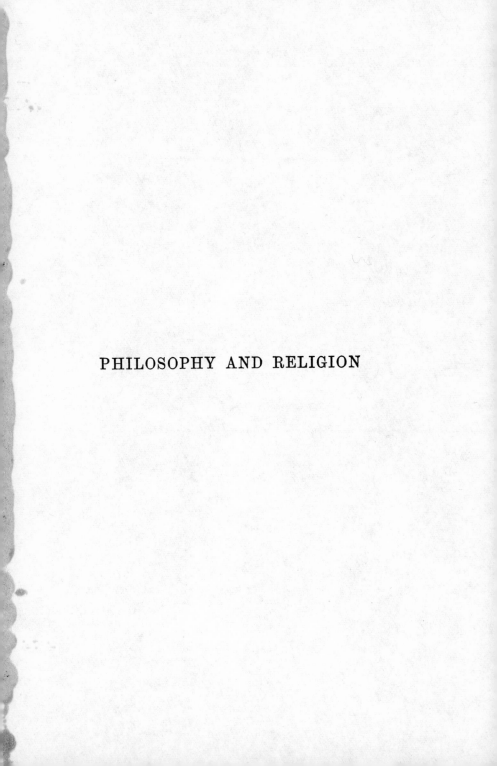

PHILOSOPHY AND RELIGION

PHILOSOPHY AND RELIGION

SIX LECTURES
DELIVERED AT CAMBRIDGE

BY

HASTINGS RASHDALL

D. LITT. (OXON.), D.C.L. (DUNELM.)

FELLOW OF THE BRITISH ACADEMY
FELLOW AND TUTOR OF NEW COLLEGE, OXFORD

GREENWOOD PRESS, PUBLISHERS
WESTPORT, CONNECTICUT

Originally published in 1910
by Charles Scribner's Sons, New York

Reprinted from a copy in the collections
of the Brooklyn Public Library

First Greenwood Reprinting 1970

Library of Congress Catalogue Card Number 79-98791

SBN 8371-3025-5

PRINTED IN UNITED STATES OF AMERICA

GENERAL INTRODUCTION
TO THE SERIES

MAN has no deeper or wider interest than theology;
none deeper, for however much he may change, he
never loses his love of the many questions it covers;
and none wider, for under whatever law he may live
he never escapes from its spacious shade; nor does
he ever find that it speaks to him in vain or uses a
voice that fails to reach him.   Once the present
writer was talking with a friend who has equal fame
as a statesman and a man of letters, and he said,
'Every day I live, Politics, which are affairs of
Man and Time, interest me less, while Theology,
which is an affair of God and Eternity, interests me
more.' As with him, so with many, though the many
feel that their interest is in theology and not in dogma.
Dogma, they know, is but a series of resolutions
framed by a council or parliament, which they do
not respect any the more because the parliament was
composed of ecclesiastically-minded persons; while the
theology which so interests them is a discourse touching God, though the Being so named is the God man
conceived as not only related to himself and his world
but also as rising ever higher with the notions of the
self and the world.   Wise books, not in dogma but in
theology, may therefore be described as the supreme

need of our day, for only such can save us from much
fanaticism and secure us in the full possession of a
sober and sane reason.

Theology is less a single science than an encyclopædia of sciences; indeed all the sciences which
have to do with man have a better right to be called
theological than anthropological, though the man it
studies is not simply an individual but a race.   Its
way of viewing man is indeed characteristic; from this
have come some of its brighter ideals and some of its
darkest dreams.   The ideals are all either ethical or
social, and would make of earth a heaven, creating
fraternity amongst men and forming all states into a
goodly sisterhood; the dreams may be represented by
doctrines which concern sin on the one side and the
will of God on the other.   But even this will cannot
make sin luminous, for were it made radiant with
grace, it would cease to be sin.

These books then,—which have all to be written by
men who have lived in the full blaze of modern light,
—though without having either their eyes burned
out or their souls scorched into insensibility,—are intended to present God in relation to Man and Man
in relation to God.   It is intended that they begin, not
in date of publication, but in order of thought, with a
Theological Encyclopædia which shall show the circle
of sciences co-ordinated under the term Theology,
though all will be viewed as related to its central or
main idea.   This relation of God to human knowledge will then be looked at through mind as a communion of Deity with humanity, or God in fellowship

with concrete man. On this basis the idea of Revelation will be dealt with. Then, so far as history and philology are concerned, the two Sacred Books, which are here most significant, will be viewed as the scholar, who is also a divine, views them; in other words, the Old and New Testaments, regarded as human documents, will be criticised as a literature which expresses relations to both the present and the future; that is, to the men and races who made the books, as well as to the races and men the books made. The Bible will thus be studied in the Semitic family which gave it being, and also in the Indo-European families which gave to it the quality of the life to which they have attained. But Theology has to do with more than sacred literature; it has also to do with the thoughts and life its history occasioned. Therefore the Church has to be studied and presented as an institution which God founded and man administers. But it is possible to know this Church only through the thoughts it thinks, the doctrines it holds, the characters and the persons it forms, the people who are its saints and embody its ideals of sanctity, the acts it does, which are its sacraments, and the laws it follows and enforces, which are its polity, and the young it educates and the nations it directs and controls. These are the points to be presented in the volumes which follow, which are all to be occupied with theology or the knowledge of God and His ways.

A. M. F.

'O.'

PREFACE

THESE Lectures were delivered in Cambridge during the Lent Term of last year, on the invitation of a Committee presided over by the Master of Magdalene, before an audience of from three hundred to four hundred University men, chiefly Undergraduates. They were not then, and they are not now, intended for philosophers or even for beginners in the systematic study of philosophy, but as aids to educated men desirous of thinking out for themselves a reasonable basis for personal Religion.

The Lectures—especially the first three—deal with questions on which I have already written. I am indebted to the Publisher of *Contentio Veritatis* and the other contributors to that volume for raising no objection to my publishing Lectures which might possibly be regarded as in part a condensation, in part an expansion of my Essay on 'The ultimate basis of Theism.' I have dealt more systematically with many of the problems here discussed in an Essay upon 'Personality in God and Man' contributed to *Personal Idealism* (edited by Henry

Sturt) and in my 'Theory of Good and Evil.'
Some of the doctrinal questions touched on in
Lecture VI. have been more fully dealt with in
my volume of University Sermons, *Doctrine and
Development*.

Questions which were asked at the time and
communications which have since reached me have
made me feel, more even than I did when I was
writing the Lectures, how inadequate is the treatment here given to many great problems. On some
matters much fuller explanation and discussion will
naturally be required to convince persons previously
unfamiliar with Metaphysic : on others it is the more
advanced student of Philosophy who will complain
that I have only touched upon the fringe of a vast
subject. But I have felt that I could not seriously
expand any part of the Lectures without changing
the whole character of the book, and I have been
compelled in general to meet the demand for further
explanation only by the above general reference to
my other books, by the addition of a few notes, and
by appending to each chapter some suggestions for
more extended reading. These might of course
have been indefinitely enlarged, but a long list of
books is apt to defeat its own purpose : people with
a limited time at their disposal want to know which
book to make a beginning upon.

The Lectures are therefore published for the most

part just as they were delivered, in the hope that they may suggest lines of thought which may be intellectually and practically useful. I trust that any philosopher who may wish to take serious notice of my views—especially the metaphysical views expressed in the first few chapters—will be good enough to remember that the expression of them is avowedly incomplete and elementary, and cannot fairly be criticized in much detail without reference to my other writings.

I am much indebted for several useful suggestions and for valuable assistance in revising the proofs to one of the hearers of the Lectures, Mr. A. G. Widgery, Scholar of St. Catherine's College, Cambridge, now Lecturer in University College, Bristol.

H. RASHDALL.

NEW COLLEGE, OXFORD,
Jan. 6, 1909.

CONTENTS

LECTURE I

LECTURE II

xii

LECTURE III

LECTURE V

1. There is no special organ of religious knowledge, but religious knowledge has many characteristics which may be conveniently suggested by the use of the term 'faith,' especially its connexion with character and Will.

LECTURE VI

PHILOSOPHY AND RELIGION

LECTURE I

MIND AND MATTER

I HAVE been invited to speak to you about the relations between Religion and Philosophy. To do that in a logical and thoroughgoing way it would be necessary to discuss elaborately the meaning first of Religion and then of Philosophy. Such a discussion would occupy at least a lecture, and I am unwilling to spend one out of six scanty hours in formal preliminaries. I shall assume, therefore, that we all know in some general way the meaning of Religion. It is not necessary for our present purpose to discuss such questions as the definition of Religion for purposes of sociological investigation, or the possibility of a Religion without a belief in God, or the like. I shall assume that, whatever else may be included in the term Religion, Christianity may at least be included in it; and that what you are practically most interested in is the bearing of Philosophy upon the Christian ideas concerning the

being and nature of God, the hope of Immortality,
the meaning and possibility of Revelation. When
we turn to Philosophy, I cannot perhaps assume
with equal confidence that all of you know what it
is. But then learning what Philosophy is—especially that most fundamental part of Philosophy
which is called Metaphysics—is like learning to swim :
you never discover how to do it until you find yourself considerably out of your depth. You must
strike out boldly, and at last you discover what you
are after. I shall presuppose that in a general way
you do all know that Philosophy is an enquiry into
the ultimate nature of the Universe at large, as
opposed to the discussion of those particular aspects
or departments of it which are dealt with by the
special Sciences. What you want to know, I take
it, is—what rational enquiry, pushed as far as it
will go, has to say about those ultimate problems
of which the great historical Religions likewise
profess to offer solutions. The nature and scope
of Philosophy is best understood by examples : and
therefore I hope you will excuse me if without
further preface I plunge *in medias res.* I shall
endeavour to presuppose no previous acquaintance
with technical Philosophy, and I will ask those who
have already made some serious study of Philosophy
kindly to remember that I am trying to make
myself intelligible to those who have not. I shall

not advance anything which I should not be prepared to defend even before an audience of metaphysical experts. But I cannot undertake in so
short a course of lectures to meet all the objections
which will, I know, be arising in the minds of any
metaphysically trained hearers who may honour
me with their presence, many of which may probably
occur to persons not so trained. And I further
trust the Metaphysicians among you will forgive
me if, in order to be intelligible to all, I sometimes
speak with a little less than the ἀκρίβεια at which
I might feel bound to aim if I were reading a paper
before an avowedly philosophical Society. Reserva-
tions, qualifications, and elaborate distinctions must
be omitted, if I am to succeed in saying anything
clearly in the course of six lectures.

Moreover, I would remark that, though I do not
believe that an intention to edify is any excuse for
slipshod thought or intellectual dishonesty, I am
speaking now mainly from the point of view of
those who are enquiring into metaphysical truth
for the guidance of their own religious and practical
life, rather than from the point of view of pure
speculation. I do not, for my own part, believe in
any solution of the religious problem which evades
the ultimate problems of all thought. The Philosophy of Religion is for me not so much a special
and sharply distinguished branch or department of

Philosophy as a particular aspect of Philosophy in general.   But many questions which may be of much importance from the point of view of a complete theory of the Universe can be entirely, or almost entirely, put on one side when the question is, ' What may I reasonably believe about those ulti- mate questions which have a direct and immediate bearing upon my religious and moral life; what may I believe about God and Duty, about the world and its ultimate meaning, about the soul and its destiny? ' For such purposes solutions stopping short of what will fully satisfy the legitimate demands of the professed Metaphysician may be all that is neces- sary, or at least all that is possible for those who are not intending to make a serious and elaborate study of Metaphysic. I have no sympathy with the attempt to base Religion upon anything but honest enquiry into truth : and yet the professed Philosophers are just those who will most readily recognize that there are—if not what are technically called degrees of truth—still different levels of thought, different degrees of adequacy and systematic completeness, even within the limits of thoroughly philosophical thinking. I shall assume that you are not content to remain at the level of ordinary un- reflecting Common-sense or of merely traditional Religion—that you do want (so far as time and opportunity serve) to get to the bottom of things,

but that you will be content in such a course as the
present if I can suggest to you, or help you to form
for yourselves, an outline—what Plato would call
the ὑποτύπωσις of a theory of the Universe which
may still fall very far short of a finished and fully
articulated metaphysical system.

I suppose that to nearly everybody who sets himself down to think seriously about the riddle of the
Universe there very soon occurs the question whether
Materialism may not contain the solution of all
difficulties. I think, therefore, our present investigation had better begin with an enquiry whether
Materialism can possibly be true. I say 'can be
true' rather than 'is true,' because, though dogmatic
Materialists are rare, the typical Agnostic is one
who is at least inclined to admit the possibility of
Materialism, even when he does not, at the bottom
of his mind, practically assume its truth. The man
who is prepared to exclude even this one theory of
the Universe from the category of possible but
unprovable theories is not, properly speaking, an
Agnostic. To know that Materialism at least is not
true is to know something, and something very
important, about the ultimate nature of things. I
shall not attempt here any very precise definition
of what is meant by Materialism. Strictly speaking,
it ought to mean the view that nothing really exists
but matter. But the existence, in some sense or

other, of our sensations and thoughts and emotions is so obvious to Common-sense that such a creed can hardly be explicitly maintained : it is a creed which is refuted in the very act of enunciating it. For practical purposes, therefore, Materialism may be said to be the view that the ultimate basis of all existence is matter ; and that thought, feeling, emotion—consciousness of every kind—is merely an effect, a by-product or concomitant, of certain material processes.

Now if we are to hold that matter is the only thing which exists, or is the ultimate source of all that exists, we ought to be able to say what matter is. To the unreflecting mind matter seems to be the thing that we are most certain of, the one thing that we know all about. Thought, feeling, will, it may be suggested, are in some sense appearances which (though *we* can't help having them) might, from the point of view of superior insight, turn out to be mere delusions, or at best entirely unimportant and inconsiderable entities. This attitude of mind has been amusingly satirised by the title of one of Mr. Bradley's philosophical essays—' on the supposed uselessness of the Soul.' [1] In this state of mind matter presents itself as the one solid reality—as something undeniable, something perfectly intelligible, something, too, which is pre-eminently

1 *Mind,* vol. iv. (N.S.), 1895.

important and respectable; while thinking and feeling and willing, joy and sorrow, hope and aspiration, goodness and badness, if they cannot exactly be got rid of altogether, are, as it were, negligible quantities, which must not be allowed to disturb or interfere with the serious business of the Universe.

From this point of view matter is supposed to be the one reality with which we are in immediate contact, which we see and touch and taste and handle every hour of our lives. It may, therefore, sound a rather startling paradox to say that matter —matter in the sense of the Materialist—is something which nobody has ever seen, touched, or handled. Yet that is the literal and undeniable fact. Nobody has ever seen or touched or otherwise come in contact with a piece of matter. For in the experience which the plain man calls seeing or touching there is always present another thing. Even if we suppose that he is justified in saying 'I touch matter,' there is always present the 'I' as well as the matter.[1] It is always and inevitably matter + mind that he knows. Nobody ever can get away from this 'I,' nobody can ever see or feel what matter is like apart from the 'I' which knows

---

[1] I do not mean of course that in the earliest stages of consciousness this distinction is actually made; but, if there are stages of consciousness in which the 'I' is not realized, the idea of matter or even of an 'object' or 'not-self' existing apart from consciousness must be supposed to be equally absent.

it. He may, indeed, infer that this matter exists
apart from the ' I ' which knows it. He may infer
that it exists, and may even go as far as to assume
that, apart from his seeing or touching, or anybody
else's seeing or touching, matter possesses all those
qualities which it possesses for his own consciousness.
But this is inference, and not immediate knowledge.
And the validity or reasonableness of the inference
may be disputed. How far it is reasonable or
legitimate to attribute to matter as it is in itself
the qualities which it has for us must depend upon
the nature of those qualities. Let us then go on to
ask whether the qualities which constitute matter
as we know it are qualities which we can reasonably
or even intelligibly attribute to a supposed matter-
in-itself, to matter considered as something capable
of existing by itself altogether apart from any
kind of conscious experience.

In matter, as we know it, there are two elements.
There are certain sensations, or certain qualities
which we come to know by sensation, and there are
certain relations. Now, with regard to the sensations, a very little reflection will, I think, show us
that it is absolutely meaningless to say that matter
has the qualities implied by these sensations, even
when they are not felt, and would still possess them,
even supposing it never had been and never woud
be felt by any one whatever. In a world in which

there were no eyes and no minds, what would be
the meaning of saying that things were red or blue ?
In a world in which there were no ears and no minds,
there would clearly be no such thing as sound. This
is exactly the point at which Locke's analysis stopped.
He admitted that the 'secondary qualities'—colours,
sounds, tastes—of objects were really not in the
things themselves but in the mind which perceives
them. What existed in the things was merely
a power of producing these sensations in us, the
quality in the thing being not in the least like the
sensations which it produces in us : he admitted
that this power of producing a sensation was something different from, and totally unlike, the sensation
itself. But when he came to the primary qualities—
solidity, shape, magnitude and the like—he supposed
that the qualities in the thing were exactly the same
as they are for our minds. If all mind were to
disappear from the Universe, there would henceforth
be no red and blue, no hot and cold ; but things would
still be big or small, round or square, solid or fluid.
Yet, even with these 'primary qualities' the reference to mind is really there just as much as in the
case of the secondary qualities ; only the fact is not
quite so obvious. And one reason for this is that
these primary qualities involve, much more glaringly
and unmistakably than the secondary, something
which is not *mere* sensation—something which

implies thought and not mere sense. What do we
mean by solidity, for instance ? We mean partly
that we get certain sensations from touching the
object—sensations of touch and sensations of what
is called the muscular sense, sensations of muscular
exertion and of pressure resisted. Now, so far as
that is what solidity means, it is clear that the
quality in question involves as direct a reference to
our subjective feelings as the secondary qualities of
colour and sound. But something more than this
is implied in our idea of solidity. We think of
external objects as occupying space. And speciality
cannot be analysed away into mere feelings of ours.
The feelings of touch which we derive from an object
come to us one after the other. No mental reflection
upon sensations which come one after the other in
time could ever give us the idea of space, if they were
not spacially related from the first. It is of the
essence of speciality that the parts of the object
shall be thought of as existing side by side, outside
one another. But this side-by-sideness, this out-
sideness, is after all a way in which the things present
themselves to a mind. Space is made up of relations ;
and what is the meaning of relations apart from a
mind which relates, or *for* which the things are
related ? If speciality were a quality of the thing
in itself, it would exist no matter what became of
other things. It would be quite possible, therefore,

that the top of this table should exist without the bottom : yet everybody surely would admit the meaninglessness of talking about a piece of matter (no matter how small, be it an atom or the smallest electron conceived by the most recent physical speculation) which had a top without a bottom, or a right-hand side without a left. This space-occupying quality which is the most fundamental element in our ordinary conception of matter is wholly made up of the relation of one part of it to another. Now can a relation exist except for a mind ? As it seems to me, the suggestion is meaning-less. Relatedness only has a meaning when thought of in connection with a mind which is capable of grasping or holding together both terms of the relation. The relation between point A and point B is not *in* point A or *in* point B taken by themselves. It is all in the ' between ' : ' betweenness ' from its very nature cannot exist in any one point of space or in several isolated points of space or things in space ; it must exist only in some one existent which holds together and connects those points. And nothing, as far as we can understand, can do that except a mind. Apart from mind there can be no relatedness : apart from relatedness no space : apart from space no matter. It follows that apart from mind there can be no matter.

It will probably be known to all of you that the

first person to make this momentous inference was Bishop Berkeley. There was, indeed, an obscure medieval schoolman, hardly recognized by the historians of Philosophy, one Nicholas of Autrecourt, Dean of Metz,[1] who anticipated him in the fourteenth century, and other better-known schoolmen who approximated to the position; and there are, of course, elements in the teaching of Plato and even of Aristotle, or possible interpretations of Plato and Aristotle, which point in the same direction. But full-blown Idealism, in the sense which involves a denial of the independent existence of matter, is always associated with the name of Bishop Berkeley.

I can best make my meaning plain to you by quoting a passage or two from his *Principles of Human Knowledge*, in which he extends to the primary qualities of matter the analysis which Locke had already applied to the secondary.

'But, though it were possible that solid, figured, moveable substances may exist without the mind, corresponding to the ideas we have of bodies, yet how is it possible for us to know this? Either we must know it by Sense or by Reason.—As for our senses, by them we have the knowledge only of our sensations, ideas, or those things that are immediately perceived by sense, call them what you will: but they do not inform us that things exist

---

[1] I have dealt at length with this forgotten thinker in a Presidential Address to the Aristotelian Society, printed in their *Proceedings* for 1907.

without the mind, or unperceived, like to those which are perceived. This the Materialists themselves acknowledge.—It remains therefore that if we have any knowledge at all of external things, it must be by Reason inferring their existence from what is immediately perceived by sense. But what reason can induce us to believe the existence of bodies without the mind, from what we perceive, since the very patrons of Matter themselves do not pretend there is any *necessary* connexion betwixt them and our ideas? I say it is granted on all hands—and what happens in dreams, frenzies, and the like, puts it beyond dispute—that it is possible we might be affected with all the ideas we have now, though there were no bodies existing without resembling them. Hence, it is evident the supposition of external bodies is not necessary for the producing our ideas; since it is granted they are produced sometimes, and might possibly be produced always in the same order we see them in at present, without their concurrence.

*   *   *   *   *   *

'In short, if there were external bodies, it is impossible we should ever come to know it; and if there were not, we might have the very same reasons to think there were that we have now. Suppose—what no one can deny possible—an intelligence *without the help of external bodies*, to be affected with the same train of sensations or ideas that you are, imprinted in the same order and with like vividness in his mind. I ask whether that intelligence hath not all the reason to believe the existence of corporeal substances, represented by his ideas, and exciting them in his mind, that you can possibly have for believing the same thing? Of this there can be no

question—which one consideration were enough to make
any reasonable person suspect the strength of whatever
arguments he may think himself to have, for the existence of bodies without the mind.'[1]

Do you say that in that case the tables and chairs
must be supposed to disappear the moment we all
leave the room ?   It is true that we do commonly
think of the tables and chairs as remaining, even
when there is no one there to see or touch them.
But that only means, Berkeley explains, that if we
or any one else were to come back into the room,
we should perceive them.   Moreover, even in thinking of them as things which might be perceived
under certain conditions, they have entered our
minds and so proclaimed their ideal or mind-implying
character.   To prove that things exist without the
mind we should have to conceive of things as unconceived or unthought of.   And that is a feat
which no one has ever yet succeeded in accomplishing.

Here is Berkeley's own answer to the objection :

'But, say you, surely there is nothing easier than for
me to imagine trees, for instance, in a park, or books
existing in a closet, and nobody by to perceive them.   I
answer, you may so, there is no difficulty in it; but
what is all this, I beseech you, more than framing in your
mind certain ideas which you call books and trees, and

---

[1] *Principles of Human Knowledge*, pt. i., §§ 18, 20.

at the same time omitting to frame the idea of any one
that may perceive them? But do not you yourself perceive or think of them all the while? This therefore is
nothing to the purpose : it only shews you have the
power of imagining or forming ideas in your mind ; but
it does not shew that you can conceive it possible the
objects of your thought may exist without the mind.
To make out this, it is necessary that *you* conceive them
existing unconceived or unthought of, which is a mani-
fest repugnancy. When we do our utmost to conceive
the existence of external bodies, we are all the while only
contemplating our own ideas. But the mind, *taking no
notice of itself*, is deluded to think it can and does conceive bodies existing unthought of or without the mind,
though at the same time they are apprehended by, or
exist in, itself. A little attention will discover to any one
the truth and evidence of what is here said, and make it
unnecessary to insist on any other proofs against the
existence of *material substance.*' [1]

Berkeley no doubt did not adequately appreciate
the importance of the distinction between mere
sensations and mental relations. In the paragraph
which I have read to you he tends to explain space
away into mere subjective feelings : in this respect
and in many others he has been corrected by Kant
and the post-Kantian Idealists. Doubtless we
cannot analyse away our conception of space or of
substance into mere feelings. But relations imply
mind no less than sensations. Things are no mere

[1] *Principles of Human Knowledge*, pt. i., § 23.

bundles of sensations; we do think of them as
objects or substances possessing attributes. Indeed
to call them (with Berkeley), 'bundles of sensations'
implies that the bundle is as important an element
in thinghood as the sensations themselves. The
bundle implies what Kant would call the intellectual
'categories' of Substance, Quantity, Quality, and
the like. We do think objects: but an object is
still an object of thought. We can attach no intelligible meaning to the term 'object' which does not
imply a subject.

If there is nothing in matter, as we know it, which
does not obviously imply mind, if the very idea of
matter is unintelligible apart from mind, it is clear
that matter can never have existed without mind.

What then, it may be asked, of the things which
no human eye has ever seen or even thought of?
Are we to suppose that a new planet comes into
existence for the first time when first it sails into the
telescope of the astronomer, and that Science is
wrong in inferring that it existed not only before
that particular astronomer saw it, but before there
were any astronomers or other human or even animal
intelligences upon this planet to observe it? Did
the world of Geology come into existence for the
first time when some eighteenth-century geologist
first suspected that the world was more than six
thousand years old? Are all those ages of past

history, when the earth and the sun were but nebulæ,
a mere imagination, or did that nebulous mass come
into existence thousands or millions of years afterwards when Kant or Laplace first conceived that
it had existed ? The supposition is clearly self-
contradictory and impossible. If Science be not
a mass of illusion, this planet existed millions of
years before any human—or, so far as we know,
any animal minds—existed to think its existence.
And yet I have endeavoured to show the absurdity
of supposing that matter can exist except for a mind.
It is clear, then, that it cannot be merely for such
minds as ours that the world has always existed.
Our minds come and go. They have a beginning ;
they go to sleep ; they may, for aught that we can
immediately know, come to an end. At no time does
any one of them, at no time do all of them together,
apprehend all that there is to be known. We do not
create a Universe ; we discover it piece by piece,
and after all very imperfectly. Matter cannot
intelligibly be supposed to exist apart from Mind :
and yet it clearly does not exist merely for *our* minds.
Each of us knows only one little bit of the Universe :
all of us together do not know the whole. If the
whole is to exist at all, there must be some one mind
which knows the whole. The mind which is necessary to the very existence of the Universe is the
mind that we call God.

In this way we are, as it seems to me, led up by a train of reasoning which is positively irresistible to the idea that, so far from matter being the only existence, it has no existence of its own apart from some mind which knows it—in which and for which it exists. The existence of a Mind possessing universal knowledge is necessary as the presupposition· both of there being any world to know, and also of there being any lesser minds to know it. It is, indeed, possible to believe in the eternal existence of limited minds, while denying the existence of the one Omniscient Mind. That is a hypothesis on which I will say a word hereafter.[1] It is enough here to say that it is one which is not required to explain the world as we know it. The obvious *prima facie* view of the matter is that the minds which apparently have a beginning, which develope slowly and gradually and in close connexion with certain physical processes, owe their origin to whatever is the ultimate source or ground of the physical processes themselves. The order or systematic interconnexion of all the observable phenomena in the Universe suggests that the ultimate Reality must be one Being of some kind; the argument which I have suggested leads us to regard that one Reality as a spiritual Reality. We are not yet entitled to speak of this physical Universe as *caused*

[1] See Lecture IV., pp. 96-101, 123-6.

by God : that is a question which I hope to discuss in our next lecture. All that I want to establish now is that we cannot explain the world without the supposition of one universal Mind in which and for which all so-called material things exist, and always have existed.

So far I have endeavoured to establish the existence of God by a line of thought which also leads to the position that matter has no independent existence apart from conscious mind, that at bottom nothing exists except minds and their experiences. Now I know that this is a line of thought which, to those who are unfamiliar with it, seems so paradoxical and extravagant that, even when a man does not see his way to reply to it, it will seldom produce immediate or permanent conviction the first time he becomes acquainted with it. It is for the most part only by a considerable course of habituation, extending over some years, that a man succeeds in thinking himself into the idealistic view of the Universe. And after all, there are many minds—some of them, I must admit, not wanting in philosophical power—who never succeed in accomplishing that feat at all. Therefore, while I feel bound to assert that the clearest and most irrefragable argument for the existence of God is that which is supplied by the idealistic line of thought, I should be sorry to have to admit that a man

cannot be a Theist, or that he cannot be a Theist
on reasonable grounds, without first being an Idealist.
From my own point of view most of the other reasons
for believing in the existence of God resolve themselves into idealistic arguments imperfectly thought
out.   But they may be very good arguments, as far
as they go, even when they are not thought out to
what seem to me their logical consequences.   One
of these lines of thought I shall hope to develope in
my next lecture ; but meanwhile let me attempt
to reduce the argument against Materialism to a
form in which it will perhaps appeal to Common-
sense without much profound metaphysical reflection.

At the level of ordinary common-sense thought
there appear to be two kinds of Reality—mind and
matter.   And yet our experience of the unity of
Nature, of the intimate connexion between human
and animal minds and their organisms (organisms
governed by a single intelligible and interconnected
system of laws) is such that we can hardly help
regarding them as manifestations or products or
effects or aspects of some one Reality.   There is,
almost obviously, some kind of Unity underlying
all the diversity of things.   Our world does not
arise by the coming together of two quite independent
Realities—mind and matter—governed by no law
or by unconnected and independent systems of law.

All things, all phenomena, all events form parts of
a single inter-related, intelligible whole : that is the
presupposition not only of Philosophy but of Science.
Or if any one chooses to say that it *is* a presupposition and so an unwarrantable piece of dogmatism,
I will say that it is the hypothesis to which all our
knowledge points.   It is at all events the one
common meeting-point of nearly all serious thinkers.
The question remains, ' What is the nature of this
one Reality ? ' Now, if this ultimate Reality be
not mind, it must be one of two things.   It must
be matter, or it must be a third thing which is neither
mind nor matter, but something quite different from
either.   Now many who will not follow the idealistic
line of thought the whole way—so far as to recognize
that the ultimate Reality is Mind—will at least
admit that Idealists have successfully shown the
impossibility of supposing that the ultimate Reality
can be matter.   For all the properties of matter
are properties which imply some relation to our
sensibility or our thought.   Moreover, there is such
a complete heterogeneity between consciousness
and unconscious matter, considered as something
capable of existing without mind, that it seems
utterly impossible and unthinkable that mind should
be simply the product or attribute of matter.   That
the ultimate Reality cannot be what we mean by
matter has been admitted by the most naturalistic,

and, in the ordinary sense, anti-religious thinkers—
Spinoza, for instance, and Haeckel, and Herbert
Spencer. The question remains, ' Which is the
easier, the more probable, the more reasonable
theory—that the ultimate Reality should be Mind,
or that it should be something so utterly unintelligible
and inconceivable to us as a *tertium quid*—a mysterious Unknown and Unknowable—which is neither
mind nor matter ? ' For my own part, I see no
reason to suppose that our inability to think of anything which is neither matter nor mind but quite
unlike either is a mere imperfection of human
thought. It seems more reasonable to assume that
our inability to think of such a mysterious X is
due to there being no such thing.[1]

Our only way of judging of the Unknown is by
the analogy of the known. It is more probable,
surely, that the world known to us should exhibit
something of the characteristics of the Reality from
which it is derived, or of which it forms a manifes-
tation, than that it should exhibit none of these
characteristics. No doubt, if we were to argue from
some small part of our experience, or from the
detailed characteristics of one part of our experience
to what is beyond our experience ; if, for instance

[1] I have attempted to meet this line of argument somewhat more
adequately, in the form in which it has recently been taken up by
Professor Höffding in his *Philosophy of Religion*, in a review in the
Review of Theology and Philosophy for November, 1907 (vol. iii.).

(I am here replying to an objection of Höffding's), a blind man were to argue that the world must be colourless because he sees no colour, or if any of us were to affirm that in other planets there can be no colours but what we see, no sensations but what we feel, no mental powers but what we possess, the inference would be precarious enough. The Anthropomorphist in the strict sense—the man who thinks that God or the gods must have human bodies—no doubt renders himself liable to the gibe that, if oxen could think, they would imagine the gods to be like oxen, and so on. But the cases are not parallel. We have no difficulty in thinking that in other worlds there may be colours which we have never seen, or whole groups of sensation different from our own : we cannot think that any existence should be neither mind nor matter, but utterly unlike either. We are not arguing from the mere absence of some special experience, but from the whole character of *all* the thought and experience that we actually possess, of all that we are and the whole Universe with which we are in contact. The characteristic of the whole world which we know is that it consists of mind and matter in close connexion—we may waive for a moment the nature of that connexion. Is it more probable that the ultimate Reality which lies beyond our reach should be something which possesses the characteristics of mind, or that it should be totally unlike either mind or matter ? Do you insist that we logically ought to say it might contain the characteristics of both mind and matter ? There is only one way in which such a combination seems clearly thinkable by us, *i.e.* when we represent matter as either in the idealistic sense the thought or experience of mind, or (after the fashion of ordinary realistic Theism) as created or produced by mind. But if you insist on something more than this, if you want to think of the qualities of matter as in some other way included in the nature of the ultimate Reality as well as those of mind, at all events we could still urge that we shall get nearer to the truth by thinking of this ultimate Reality in its mind-aspect than by thinking of it in its matter-aspect.

I do not believe that the human mind is really equal to the task of thinking of a Reality which is one and yet is neither mind nor matter but something which combines the nature of both. Practically, where such a creed is professed, the man either thinks of an unconscious Reality in some way generating or evolving mind, and so falls back into the Materialism which he has verbally disclaimed ; or he thinks of a mind producing or causing or generating a matter which when produced is something different from itself. This last is of course ordinary Theism in the form in which it is commonly

held by those who are not Idealists. From a
practical and religious point of view there is nothing
to be said against such a view. Still it involves a
Dualism, the philosophical difficulties of which I
have attempted to suggest to you. I confess that
for my own part the only way in which I can conceive of a single ultimate Reality which combines
the attributes of what we call mind with those of
what we know as matter is by thinking of a Mind
conscious of a world or nature which has no existence except in and for that Mind and whatever
less complete consciousnesses that may be. I trust
that those who have failed to follow my sketch of
the arguments which lead to this idealistic conclusion may at least be led by it to see the difficulties either of Materialism or of that kind of
agnostic Pantheism which, while admitting in words
that the ultimate Reality is not matter, refuses to
invest it with the attributes of mind. The argument may be reduced to its simplest form by saying
we believe that the ultimate Reality is Mind because
mind will explain matter, while matter will not
explain mind: while the idea of a Something which
is neither in mind nor matter is both unintelligible
and gratuitous.

And this line of thought may be supplemented by
another. Whatever may be thought of the existence of matter apart from mind, every one will

admit that matter possesses no value or worth apart from mind.   When we bring into account our moral judgements or judgements of value, we have no difficulty in recognizing mind as the highest or best kind of existence known to us.   There is, surely, a certain intrinsic probability in supposing that the Reality from which all being is derived must possess at least as much worth or value as the derived being ; and that in thinking of that Reality by the analogy of the highest kind of existence known to us we shall come nearer to a true thought of it than by any other way of thinking possible to us.   This is a line of argument which I hope to develope further when I come to examine the bearing upon the religious problem of what is as real a part of our experience as any other—our moral experience.

I will remind you in conclusion, that our argument for the existence of God is at present incomplete. I have tried to lead you to the idea that the ultimate Reality is spiritual, that it is a Mind which knows, or is conscious of, matter.   I have tried to lead you with the Idealist to think of the physical Universe as having no existence except in the mind of God, or at all events (for those who fail to follow the idealistic line of thought) to believe that the Universe does not exist without such a Mind.   What further relation exists between physical nature and this Universal Spirit, I shall hope in the next lecture

to consider ; and in so doing to suggest a line of
argument which will independently lead to the same
result, and which does not necessarily presuppose
the acceptance of the idealistic creed.

LITERATURE

The reader who wishes to have the idealistic argument
sketched in the foregoing chapter developed more fully
should read Berkeley's *Principles of Human Knowledge.*
For the correction of Berkeley's sensationalistic mistakes the
best course is to read Kant's *Critique of Pure Reason* or the
shorter *Prolegomena to any future Metaphysic* or any of the
numerous expositions or commentaries upon Kant. (One
of the best is the 'Reproduction' prefixed to Dr. Hutchison
Stirling's *Text-book to Kant.*) The non-metaphysical reader
should, however, be informed that Kant is very hard reading,
and is scarcely intelligible without some slight knowledge of the
previous history of Philosophy, especially of Locke, Berkeley,
and Hume, while some acquaintance with elementary Logic is
also desirable. He will find the argument for non-sensa-
tionalistic Idealism re-stated in a post-Kantian but much
easier form in Ferrier's *Institutes of Metaphysic.* The argument for a theistic Idealism is powerfully stated (though it is
not easy reading) in the late Prof. T. H. Green's *Prolegomena
to Ethics,* Book I. In view of recent realistic revivals I may
add that the earlier chapters of Mr. Bradley's *Appearance
and Reality* still seem to me to contain an unanswerable
defence of Idealism as against Materialism or any form of
Realism, though his Idealism is not of the theistic type
defended in the above lecture. The idealistic argument is
stated in a way which makes strongly for Theism by Professor
Ward in *Naturalism and Agnosticism*—a work which would
perhaps be the best sequel to these lectures for any reader

who does not want to undertake a whole course of
philosophical reading : readers entirely unacquainted with
Physical Science might do well to begin with Part II. A
more elementary and very clear defence of Theism from the
idealistic point of view is to be found in Dr. Illingworth's
Personality Human and Divine. Representatives of non-
idealistic Theism will be mentioned at the end of the next
lecture.

LECTURE II

THE UNIVERSAL CAUSE

IN my last lecture I endeavoured to show that matter, so far from constituting the ultimate Reality, cannot reasonably be thought of as existing at all without mind; and that we cannot explain the world without assuming the existence of a Mind in which and for which everything that is not mind has its being. But we are still very far from having fully cleared up the relation between the divine Mind and that Nature which exists in it and for it: while we have hardly dealt at all with the relation between the universal Mind and those lesser minds which we have treated—so far without much argument—as in some way derived from, or dependent upon, that Mind. So far as our previous line of argument goes, we might have to look upon the world as the thought of God, but not as caused by Him or due to His will. We might speak of God as 'making Nature,' but only in the sense in which you or I make Nature when we think it or experience it.

' The world is as necessary to God as God is to the world,' we are often told—for instance by my own revered teacher, the late Professor Green. How unsatisfactory this position is from a religious point of view I need hardly insist. For all that such a theory has to say to the contrary, we might have to suppose that, though God is perfectly good, the world which He is compelled to think is very bad, and going from bad to worse. To think of God merely as the Mind which eternally contemplates Nature, without having any power whatever of determining what sort of Nature it is to be, supplies no ground for hope or aspiration—still less for worship, adoration, imitation. I suggested the possibility that from such a point of view God might be thought of as good, and the world as bad. But that is really to concede too much. A being without a will could as little be bad as he could be good : he would be simply a being without a character. From an intellectual point such a way of looking at the Universe might be more intelligent or intelligible than that of pure Materialism or pure Agnosticism ; but morally and religiously I don't know that, when its consequences are fully realized, it is any great improvement upon either of them.[1]

[1] Of course deeply religious men like Green who have held this view did not admit, or did not realize, such consequences. The tendency here criticized is undoubtedly derived from Hegel, but passages suggestive of the opposite view can be extracted from his

Moreover, even intellectually it fails to satisfy the demand which most reflecting people feel, that the world shall be regarded as a Unity of some kind. If God is thought of as linked by some inexplicable fate to a Nature over which He has no sort of control—not so much control as a mere human being who can produce limited changes in the world,—we can hardly be said to have reduced the world to a Unity. The old Dualism has broken out again : after all we still have God and the world confronting one another ; neither of them is in any way explained by the other. Still less could such a world be supposed to have a purpose or rational end. For our own mere intellectual satisfaction as well as for the satisfaction of our religious needs we must go on to ask whether we are not justified in thinking of God as the Cause or Creator of the world, as well as the Thinker of it.

This enquiry introduces us to the whole problem of Causality. The sketch which I gave you last time of Bishop Berkeley's argument was a very imperfect one. Bishop Berkeley was from one point of view a great philosophic iconoclast, though he destroyed only that he might build up. He destroyed the superstition of a self-existing matter :

writings, *e.g.* : 'God, however, as subjective Power, is not simply will, intention, etc., but rather immediate Cause' (*Philosophy of Religion*, Eng. trans., ii. p. 129).

he also waged war against what I will venture to call the kindred superstition of a mysterious causal nexus between the physical antecedent and the physical consequent. On this side his work was carried on by Hume. Berkeley resolved our knowledge into a succession of ' ideas.' He did, no doubt, fall into the mistake of treating our knowledge as if it were a mere succession of feelings : he ignored far too much—though he did not do so completely—that other element in our knowledge, the element of intellectual relation, of which I said something last time. Here, no doubt, Berkeley has been corrected by Kant ; and, so far, practically all modern Idealists will own their indebtedness to Kant. Even in the apprehension of a succession of ideas, in the mere recognition that this feeling comes after that, there is an element which cannot be explained by mere feeling. The apprehension that this feeling came after that feeling is not itself a feeling. But can I detect any relation between these experiences of mine except that of succession ? We commonly speak of fire as the cause of the melting of the wax, but what do we really know about the matter ? Surely on reflection we must admit that we know nothing but this—that, so far as our experience goes, the application of fire is always followed by the melting of the wax. Where this is the case we do, from the point of view of ordinary life, speak of the one phenomenon as the cause of the other. Where we don't discover such an invariable succession, we don't think of the one event as the cause of the other.

I shall be told, perhaps, that on this view of the nature of Causality we ought to speak of night as the cause of day. So perhaps we should, if the result to which we are led by a more limited experience were not corrected by the results of a larger experience. To say nothing of the valuable correction afforded by the polar winter and the polar summer, we have learned by a more comprehensive experience to replace the law that day follows night by the wider generalisation that the visibility of objects is invariably coincident upon the presence of some luminous body and not upon a previous state of darkness. But between cases of what we call mere succession and what is commonly called causal sequence the difference lies merely in the observed fact that in some cases the sequence varies, while in others no exception has ever been discovered. No matter how frequently we observe that a sensation of red follows the impact upon the aural nerve of a shock derived from a wave of ether of such and such a length, we see no reason why it should do so. We may, no doubt, make a still wider generalization, and say that every event in Nature is invariably preceded by some definite complex of conditions,

and so arrive at a general law of the Uniformity of
Nature. And such a law is undoubtedly the express or
implied basis of all inference in the Physical Sciences.
When we have once accepted that law (as the whole
mass of our experience in the purely physical region
inclines us to do), then a single instance of A B C
being followed by D (when we are quite sure that
we have included all the antecedents which we do
not know from other experience to be irrelevant)
will warrant our concluding that we have discovered
a law of nature. On the next occasion of A B C's
occurrence we confidently predict that D will follow.
But, however often we have observed such a sequence,
and however many similar sequences we may have
observed, we are no nearer to knowing *why* D should
follow A B C : we can only know that it always
does : and on the strength of that knowledge we
infer, with a probability which we do no doubt for
practical purposes treat as a certainty, that it always
will. But on reflection we can see no reason why
a wave of ether of a certain length should produce
red rather than blue, a colour rather than a sound.
There, as always, we discover nothing but succession,
not necessary connexion

These cases of unvaried succession among phenomena, it should be observed, are quite different
from cases of real necessary connexion. We don't
want to examine thousands of instances of two

added to two to be quite sure that they always make four, nor in making the inference do we appeal to any more general law of Uniformity. We simply see that it is and always must be so. Mill no doubt tells us he has no difficulty in supposing that in the region of the fixed stars two and two might make five, but nobody believes him. At all events few of us can pretend to such feats of intellectual elasticity. No amount of contradictory testimony from travellers to the fixed stars, no matter whether they were Bishops of the highest character or trained as Professors of physical Science, would induce us to give a moment's credence to such a story. We simply see that two and two must make four, and that it is inconceivable they should ever, however exceptionally, make five. It is quite otherwise with any case of succession among external phenomena, no matter how unvaried. So long as we confine ourselves to merely physical phenomena (I put aside for the moment the case of conscious or other living beings) nowhere can we discover anything but succession ; nowhere do we discover Causality in the sense of a necessary connexion the reversal of which is inconceivable.

Are we then to conclude that there is no such thing as Causality, that in searching for a cause of everything that happens, we are pursuing a mere will o' the wisp, using a mere *vox nihili* which has

as little meaning for the reflecting mind as fate or
fortune ? Surely, in the very act of making the
distinction between succession and causality, in the
very act of denying that we can discover any causal
connexion between one physical phenomenon and
another, we imply that we have got the idea of
Causality in our minds; and that, however little
we may have discovered a genuine cause, we could
not believe that anything could happen without a
cause.

For my own part, I find it quite possible to believe
that a phenomenon which has been followed by
another phenomenon 9999 times should on the
10,000th time be followed by some other phenomenon. Give me the requisite experience, and belief
would follow; give me even any adequate evidence
that another person has had such an experience
(though I should be very particular about the
evidence), and I should find no difficulty in believing
it. But to tell me that the exception to an observed
law might take place without any cause at all for
the variation would seem to be pure nonsense.
Put the matter in another way. Let us suppose
an empty world, if one can speak of such a thing
without contradiction—let us suppose that at one
time nothing whatever had existed, neither mind
nor matter nor any of that mysterious entity which
some people find it possible to believe in which is

neither mind nor matter. Let us suppose literally nobody and nothing to have existed. Now could you under these conditions rationally suppose that anything could have come into existence ? Could you for one moment admit the possibility that after countless æons of nothingness a flash of lightning should occur or an animal be born ? Surely, on reflection those who are most suspicious of *a priori* knowledge, who are most unwilling to carry their speculations beyond the limits of actual experience, will be prepared to say, ' No, the thing is utterly for ever impossible.' *Ex nihilo nihil fit* : for every event there must be a cause. Those who profess to reject all other *a priori* or self-evident knowledge, show by their every thought and every act that they never really doubt that much.

Now, it would be just possible to contend that we have got the bare abstract concept or category of Causality in our minds, and yet that there is nothing within our experience to give it any positive content —so that we should have to say, ' Every event must have a cause, but we never know or can know what that cause is. If we are to talk about causes at all, we can only say " The Unknowable is the cause of all things." ' Such a position can be barely stated without a contradiction. But surely it is a very difficult one. Nature does not generally supply us with categories of thought, while it gives us no power or opportunity of using them. It would be like holding, for instance, that we have indeed been endowed with the idea of number in general, but that we cannot discover within our experience any numerable things; that we have got the idea of 1, 2, 3, 4, etc., but have no capacity whatever for actually counting—for saying that here are three apples, and there four marbles. And, psychologically, it would be difficult to find any parallel to anything of the kind. Nature does not first supply us with clearly defined categories of thought, and then give us a material to exercise them upon. In general we discover these abstract categories by using them in our actual thinking. We count beads or men or horses before we evolve an abstract idea of number, or an abstract multiplication table. It is very difficult to see how this idea of Cause could possibly have got into our heads if we had never in the whole course of our experience come into any sort of contact with any actual concrete cause. Where then, within our experience, if not in the succession of external events, shall we look for a cause—for something to which we can apply this category or abstract notion of causality? I answer 'We must look within : it is in our experience of volition that we actually find something answering to our idea of causal connexion.' And here, I would invite you not to think so much of our consciousness of actually moving our limbs. Here it is possible to argue plausibly that the experience of exercising causality is a delusion. I imagine that, if I will to do so, I can move my arm; but I will to stretch out my arm, and lo! it remains glued to my side, for I have suddenly been paralysed. Or I may be told that the consciousness of exerting power is a mere experience of muscular contraction, and the like. I would ask you to think rather of your power of directing the succession of your own thoughts. I am directly conscious, for instance, that the reason why I am now thinking of Causality, and not (say) of Tariff Reform, is the fact that I have conceived the design of delivering a course of lectures on this subject; the succession of ideas which flow through my mind as I write or speak is only explicable by reference to an end—an end which I am striving to bring into actual being. In such voluntarily concentrated purposeful successions of thought I am immediately exercising causality : and this causality does further influence the order of events in physical nature. My pen or my tongue moves in consequence of this striving of mine, though no doubt for such efforts to take place other physical conditions must be presupposed, which are not wholly within my own control. I am the cause, but not the whole or sole cause of these physical disturbances in external nature : I am a cause but not an uncaused cause.

My volition, though it is not the sole cause of the event which I will, is enough to give me a conception of a cause which *is* the sole cause of the events.

The attempt is of course sometimes made, as it was made by Hume, to explain away this immediate consciousness of volition, and to say that all that I immediately know is the succession of my subjective experiences. It may be contended that I don't know, any more than in the case of external phenomena, that because the thought of my lecture comes first and the thought of putting my pen into the ink to write it comes afterwards, therefore the one thought causes the other. Hence it is important to point out that I have a negative experience with which to contrast the positive experience. I do not *always*, even as regards my own inward experiences, assume that succession implies Causality. Supposing, as I speak or write, a twinge of the gout suddenly introduces itself into the succession of my experiences : then I am conscious of no such inner connexion between the new experience and that which went before it. Then I am as distinctly conscious of passivity—of not causing the succession of events which take place in my mind—as I am in the other case of actively causing it. If the consciousness of exercising activity is a delusion, why does not that delusion occur in the one case as much as in the other ? I hold then that in the consciousness of our own activity we get a real direct experience of Causality. When Causality is interpreted to mean mere necessary connexion—like the mathematical connexion between four and twice two or the logical connexion between the premisses of a Syllogism and its conclusion,—its nature is fundamentally misrepresented. The essence of Causality is not necessary connexion but Activity. Such activity we encounter in our own experience of volition and nowhere else.[1]

Now, if the only cause of which I am immediately conscious is the will of a conscious rational being, is it not reasonable to infer that some such agency is at work in the case of those phenomena which we see no reason to attribute to the voluntary actions of men and animals ? It is well known that primitive man took this step. Primitive man had no notion of the 'Uniformity of Nature' : it is only very gradually that civilized man has discovered it. But primitive man never doubted for one instant the law of Causality : he never doubted that for any change, or at least for any change of the kind which most frequently attracted his attention, there must

[1] The idea of Causality was by Kant identified with the idea of logical connexion, *i.e.* the relation of the premisses of a syllogism to its conclusion ; but this does not involve *time* at all, and time is essential to the idea of Causality. For an admirable vindication of our immediate consciousness of Causality see Professor Stout's chapter on 'The Concept of Mental Activity' in *Analytic Psychology* (Book II. chap. i.).

be a cause. Everything that moved he supposed
to be alive, or to be under the influence of some
living being more or less like himself. If the sea
raged, he supposed that the Sea-god was angry. If
it did not rain to-day, when it rained yesterday,
that was due to the favour of the Sky-god, and so on.
The world for him was full of spirits. The argument
of primitive man's unconscious but thoroughly
sound Metaphysic is well expressed by the fine
lines of Wordsworth in the *Excursion* :

> Once more to distant ages of the world
> Let us revert, and place before our thoughts
> The face which rural solitude might wear
> To the unenlightened swains of pagan Greece.
> —In that fair clime, the lonely herdsman, stretched
> On the soft grass through half a summer's day,
> With music lulled his indolent repose :
> And, in some fit of weariness, if he,
> When his own breath was silent, chanced to hear
> A distant strain, far sweeter than the sounds
> Which his poor skill could make, his fancy fetched,
> Even from the blazing chariot of the sun,
> A beardless Youth, who touched a golden lute,
> And filled the illumined groves with ravishment.
> The nightly hunter, lifting a bright eye
> Up towards the crescent moon, with grateful heart
> Called on the lovely wanderer who bestowed
> That timely light, to share his joyous sport :
> And hence, a beaming Goddess with her Nymphs,
> Across the lawn and through the darksome grove,
> (Not unaccompanied with tuneful notes
> By echo multiplied from rock or cave),

Swept in the storm of chace ; as moon and stars
Glance rapidly along the clouded heaven,
When winds are blowing strong.   The traveller slaked
His thirst from rill or gushing fount, and thanked
The Naiad.   Sunbeams, upon distant hills
Gliding apace, with shadows in their train,
Might, with small help from fancy, be transformed
Into fleet Oreads sporting visibly.
The Zephyrs fanning, as they passed, their wings,
Lacked not, for love, fair objects whom they wooed
With gentle whisper.   Withered boughs grotesque,
Stripped of their leaves and twigs by hoary age,
From depth of shaggy covert peeping forth
In the low vale, or on steep mountain side ;
And, sometimes, intermixed with stirring horns
Of the live deer, or goat's depending beard,—
These were the lurking Satyrs, a wild brood
Of gamesome Deities ; or Pan himself,
The simple shepherd's awe-inspiring God ! [1]

Growing experience of the unity of Nature, of the interdependence of all the various forces and departments of Nature, have made such a view of it impossible to civilized and educated man.   Primitive man was quite right in arguing that, where he saw motion, there must be consciousness like his own.   But we have been led by Science o believe that whatever is the cause of any one phenomenon (at least in inanimate nature), must be the cause of all.   The interconnexion, the regularity, the order observable in phenomena are too great to be the result of chance or of the undesigned concurrence of a number of

[1] *Excursion*, Book IV.

independent agencies : and perhaps we may go on
further to argue that this one cause must be the
ultimate cause even of those events which are
directly and immediately caused by our own wills.
But that is a question which I will put aside for the
present.   At least for the events of physical nature
there must be one Cause.   And if the only sort of
cause we know is a conscious and rational being,
then we have another most powerful reason for
believing that the ultimate reality, from which all
other reality is derived, is Mind—a single conscious
Mind which we may now further describe as not
only Thought or Intelligence but also Will.[1]

Let me add this additional consideration in support
of the conclusion that the world is not merely thought
by God but is also willed by God.   When we talk
about thought without will, we are talking about
something that we know absolutely nothing about.
In all the consciousness that we know of, in every
moment of our own immediate waking experience,
we find thought, feeling, willing.   Even in the
consciousness of animals there appears to be something analogous to these three sides or aspects of
consciousness : but at all events in developed human
consciousness we know of no such thing as thinking
without willing.   All thought involves attention,
and to attend is to will.   If, therefore, on the grounds

[1] For the further development of this argument see Lecture IV.

suggested by the Hegelian or other post-Kantian
Idealists, we have been led to think that the ultimate
Reality is Mind or Spirit, we should naturally con-
clude by analogy that it must be Will as well as
Thought and—I may add, though it hardly belongs
to the present argument to insist upon that—Feeling.
On the other hand if, with men like Schopenhauer
and Edouard von Hartmann,[1] we are conducted by
the appearances of design in Nature to the idea that
Nature is striving after something, that the ultimate
Reality is Will, we must supplement that line of
argument by inferring from the analogy of our own
Consciousness that Will without Reason is an unintelligible and meaningless abstraction, and that
(as indeed even Hartmann saw) Schopenhauer's
Will without Reason was as impossible an abstraction
as the apparently will-less universal Thinker of the
Hegelian :[2] while against Schopenhauer and his
more reasonable successor, Hartmann, I should insist
that an unconscious Will is as unintelligible a contradiction as an unconscious Reason. Schopenhauer
and Hegel seem to have seen, each of them, exactly

[1] See especially the earlier chapters of *The Philosophy of the Unconscious* (translated by W. C. Coupland).

[2] Of course passages can be quoted from Hegel himself which
suggest the idea that God is Will as well as Thought; I am speaking of the general tendency of Hegel and many of his disciples.
Some recent Hegelians, such as Professor Royce, seem to be less open
to this criticism, but there are difficulties in thinking of God as Will
and yet continuing to speak of ultimate Reality as out of Time.

half of the truth : God is not Will without Reason
or Reason without Will, but both Reason and Will.

And here I must try to meet an inevitable objection. I do not say that these three activities of the
human intellect stand in God side by side with the
same distinctness and (if I may say so) irreducibility
that they do in us. What feeling is for a Being who
has no material organism, we can form no distinct
conception. Our thought with its clumsy processes
of inference from the known to the unknown must
be very unlike what thought is in a Being to whom
nothing is unknown. All our thought too involves
generalization, and in universal concepts (as Mr.
Bradley has shown us) much that was present in
the living experience of actual perception is necessarily left out. Thought is but a sort of reproduction—and a very imperfect reproduction—of
actual, living, sensible experience. We cannot
suppose, then, that in God there is the same distinction between actual present experience and
the universal concepts employed in thinking which
there is in us. And so, again, willing must be a
very different thing in a being who wills or creates
the objects of his own thought from what it
is in beings who can only achieve their ends
by distinguishing in the sharpest possible manner
between the indefinite multiplicity of things which
they know but do not cause and the tiny fragment

of the Universe which by means of this knowledge
they can control. Nevertheless, though all our
thoughts of God must be inadequate, it is by thinking
of Him as Thought, Will and Feeling—emancipated
from those limitations which are obviously due to
human conditions and are inapplicable to a Universal Mind—that we shall attain to the truest knowledge of God which lies within our capacity. Do you
find a difficulty in the idea of partial and inadequate
knowledge ? Just think, then, of our knowledge
of other people's characters—of what goes on in
other people's minds. It is only by the analogy of
our own immediate experience that we can come to
know anything at all of what goes on in other people's
minds. And, after all, such insight into other
people's thoughts, emotions, motives, intentions,
characters, remains very imperfect. The difficulty
is greatest when the mind which we seek to penetrate
is far above our own. How little most of us know
what it would feel like to be a Shakespeare, a Mozart,
or a Plato ! And yet it would be absurd to talk as
if our knowledge of our fellows was no knowledge at
all. It is sufficient not merely to guide our own
thoughts and actions, but to make possible sympathy, friendship, love. Is it not so with our
knowledge of God ? The Gnosticism which forgets
the immensity of the difference between the Divine
Mind and the human is not less unreasonable—

not less opposed to the principles on which we
conduct our thinking in every other department of
life—than the Agnosticism which rejects probabilities because we cannot have immediate certainties, and insists on knowing nothing because we
cannot know everything.

The argument which infers that God is Will from
the analogy of our own consciousness is one which
is in itself independent of Idealism. It has been
used by many philosophers who are Realists, such
as Reid or Dr. Martineau, as well as by Idealists
like Berkeley, or Pfleiderer, or Lotze. It does not
necessarily presuppose Idealism ; but it does, to my
mind, fit in infinitely better with the idealistic mode
of thought than with the realistic. If you hold that
there is no difficulty in supposing dead, inert matter
to exist without any mind to think it or know it,
but that only a Mind can be supposed to cause
change or motion, you are assuming a hard and fast
distinction between matter and force which the whole
trend of modern Science is tending to break down.
It seems to imply the old Greek conception of an
inert, passive, characterless ὕλη which can only be
acted upon from without. The modern Physicist,
I imagine, knows nothing of an inert matter which
can neither attract nor repel, even if he does not
definitely embark on the more speculative theory
which actually defines the atom or the electron

as a centre of force. Activity belongs to the very essence of matter as understood by modern Science. If matter can exist without mind, there is (from the scientific point of view) some difficulty in contending that it cannot likewise move or act without being influenced by an extraneous Mind. If, on the other hand, with the Idealist we treat the notion of matter without mind as an unintelligible abstraction, that line of thought would prepare us to see in force nothing but a mode of mental action. The Idealist who has already identified matter with the object of thought will find no difficulty in going on to see in force simply the activity or expression or object of Will. And if he learns from the Physicist that we cannot in the last resort—from the physical point of view— distinguish matter from force, that will fit in very well with the metaphysical position which regards thought and will as simply two inseparable aspects of the life of mind.

And now I will return once more for a moment to the idealistic argument. I have no doubt that many of you will have felt a difficulty in accepting the position that the world with which we come in contact is merely a state of our own or anybody else's consciousness. It is so obvious that in our experi- ence we are in contact with a world which we do not create; which is what it is whether we like it or not; which opposes itself at every turn to our desires and

inclinations. You may have been convinced that
we know nothing of any external world except the
effects which it produces upon consciousness. But,
you will say to yourselves, there must have been
something to cause these effects. You are perfectly
right in so thinking. Certainly in our experience of
the world we are in contact with a Reality which is
not any state of our own mind, a Reality which we
do not create but simply discover, a Reality from
which are derived the sensations which we cannot
help feeling, and the objects which we cannot help
thinking. So far you are quite right. But very
often, when the Realist insists that there must be
something to cause in my mind this appearance,
which I call my consciousness of a table, he assumes
all the while that this something—the real table,
the table in itself—is *there*, inside or behind the
phenomenal table that I actually see and feel ; out
there, in space. But if we were right in our analysis
of space, if we were right in arguing that space is
made up of intellectual relations [1] and that intel-

---

[1] It may be objected that this is true only of 'conceptual space'
(that is, the space of Geometry), but not of 'perceptual space,' *i.e.*
space as it presents itself in a child's perception of an object. The
distinction is no doubt from many points of view important, but
we must not speak of 'conceptual space' and 'perceptual space'
as if they had nothing to do with one another. If the relations
of conceptual space were not in some sense contained or implied in
our perceptions, no amount of abstraction or reflection could get the
relations out of them.

lectual relations can have no being and no meaning
except in and for a mind which apprehends them,
then it is obvious that you must not think of this
Reality which is the cause of our experience of
external objects, as being *there*, as occupying space,
as being ' external.' If space be a form of our thought,
or (in Kantian language) a form of our sensibility,
then the Reality which is to have an existence in
itself, cannot be in space. A reality which is not in
space can no longer be thought of as matter : whatever else matter (as commonly conceived) means,
it is certainly something which occupies space.
Now we know of no kind of existence which is not
in space except Mind. On the idealistic view to
which I have been endeavouring to lead you, we
are, indeed, justified in saying that there is a Reality
which is the underlying cause or ground of our
experiences, but that that Reality is one which we
may describe as Thought no less than as Will.

It may interest some of you to know how near
one who is often considered the typical representative
of naturalistic, if not materialistic, modes of thought,
ultimately came to accepting this identification.
Let me read to you a passage from one of Mr.
Spencer's later works—the third volume of his
Sociology :—

' This transfiguration, which the inquiries of physicists
continually increase, is aided by that other transfigura-

tion resulting from metaphysical inquiries. Subjective
analysis compels us to admit that our scientific interpretations of the phenomena which objects present, are
expressed in terms of our own variously-combined sensations and ideas — are expressed, that is, in elements
belonging to consciousness, which are but symbols of the
something beyond consciousness. Though analysis
afterwards reinstates our primitive beliefs, to the extent
of showing that behind every group of phenomenal
manifestations there is always a *nexus*, which is the
reality that remains fixed amid appearances which are
variable ;[1] yet we are shown that this *nexus* of reality is
for ever inaccessible to consciousness. And when, once
more, we remember that the activities constituting consciousness, being rigorously bounded, cannot bring in
among themselves the activities beyond the bounds,
which therefore seem unconscious, though produc-
tion of either by the other seems to imply that they
are of the same essential nature ; this necessity we are
under to think of the external energy in terms of the
internal energy, gives rather a spiritualistic than a
materialistic aspect to the Universe: further thought,
however, obliging us to recognize the truth that a conception given in phenomenal manifestations of this
ultimate energy can in no wise show us what it is.'[1]

Now, I think this is one of the passages which
would justify Mr. Bradley's well-known epigram, that
Mr. Herbert Spencer has told us more about the
Unknowable than the rashest of theologians has
ever ventured to tell us about God.

[1] *Sociology*, vol. iii. p. 172.

Even Kant, who is largely responsible for the mistakes about Causality against which this lecture has been a protest—I mean the tendency to resolve it into necessary connexion—did in the end come to admit that in the large resort we come into contact with Causality only in our own Wills. I owe the reference to Professor Ward, and will quote the paragraph in which he introduces it :—

'Presentation, Feeling, Conation, are ever one insepar-able whole, and advance continuously to higher and higher forms. But for the fact that psychology was in the first instance studied, not for its own sake, but in subservience to speculation, this cardinal importance of activity would not have been so long overlooked. We should not have heard so much of passive sensations and so little of active movements. It is especially interesting to find that even Kant at length—in his latest work, the posthumous treatise on the *Connexion of Physics and Metaphysics*, only recently discovered and published— came to see the fundamental character of voluntary movement. I will venture to quote one sentence : "We should not recognise the moving forces of matter, not even through experience, if we were not conscious of our own activity in ourselves exerting acts of repulsion, approximation, etc." But to Maine de Biran, often called the French Kant, to Schopenhauer, and, finally, to our own British psychologists, Brown, Hamilton, Bain, Spencer, is especially due the merit of seeing the paramount importance of the active side of experience. To this then primarily, and not to any merely intellectual function, we may safely refer the category of causality.'[1]

I may add that Professor Ward's *Naturalism and Agnosticism*, from which I have quoted, constitutes the most brilliant and important modern defence of the doctrine which I have endeavoured very inadequately to set before you in this lecture.

It is a remarkable fact that the typical exponent of popular so-called ' scientific ' Agnosticism, and the founder of that higher metaphy ical Agnosticism which has played so large a part in the history of modern Philosophy, should before their deaths have both made confessions which really amount to an abjuration of all Agnosticism. If the ultimate Reality is to be thought of as a rational Will, analogous to the will which each of us is conscious of himself having or being, he is no longer the Unknown or the Unknowable, but the God of Religion, who has revealed Himself in the consciousness of man, ' made in the image of God.' What more about Himself we may also hold to be revealed in the human spirit, I hope to consider in our next lecture. But, meanwhile, a word may be uttered in answer to the question which may very probably be asked—Is God a Person ? A complete answer to the question would involve elaborate discussions, but for our present purpose the question may be answered very

[1] *Naturalism and Agnosticism*, vol. ii. pp. 191-2.

briefly. If we are justified in thinking of God after
the analogy of a human soul—if we are justified
in thinking of Him as a self-conscious Being who
thinks, feels, and wills, and who is, moreover (if I
may a little anticipate the subject of our next
lecture) in relation with, capable of loving and
being loved by other such beings—then it seems most
natural to speak of God's existence as personal.
For to be a self-conscious being—conscious of itself
and other beings, thinking, willing, feeling, loving—
is what we mean by being a person. If any one
prefers to speak of God as ' super-personal,' there
is no great objection to so doing, provided that
phrase is not made (as it often is) an excuse for
really thinking of God after the analogy of some
kind of existence lower than that of persons—as a
force, an unconscious substance, or merely a name
for the totality of things. But for myself, I prefer
to say that our own self-consciousness gives us only
an ideal of the highest type of existence which it
nevertheless very imperfectly satisfies, and therefore I would rather think God is a Person in a far
truer, higher, more complete sense than that in which
any human being can be a person. God alone fully
realizes the ideal of Personality. The essence of
Personality is something positive : it signifies to us
the highest kind of being within our knowledge—
not (as is too often supposed) the mere limitations

and restraints which characterize human conscious
life as we know it in ourselves. If we are justified
in thinking of God after the analogy of the highest
existence within our knowledge, we had better call
Him a Person. The word is no doubt inadequate to
the reality, as is all the language that we can employ
about God ; but it is at least more adequate than
the terms employed by those who scruple to speak
of God as a Person. It is at least more adequate
and more intelligent than to speak of Him as a force,
a substance, a 'something not ourselves which
makes for righteousness.' *Things* do not 'make for
righteousness'; and in using the term Person we
shall at least make it clear that we do not think of
Him as a 'thing,' or a collection of things, or a
vague substratum of things, or even a mere totality
of minds like our own.[1]

LITERATURE

As has been explained in this Lecture, many idealistic
writers who insist upon the necessity of God as a universal,
knowing Mind to explain both the existence of the world and
our knowledge of it, are more or less ambiguous about the
question whether the divine Mind is to be thought of as
willing or causing the world, though passages occur in the
writings of most of them which tend in this direction. 'God

[1] For a further discussion of the subject the reader may be referred
to my essay on 'Personality in God and Man' in *Personal
Idealism.*

must be thought of as creating the objects of his own thought'
is a perfectly orthodox Hegelian formula.   Among the
idealistic writers (besides Berkeley) who correct this—as it
seems to me—one-sided tendency, and who accept on the
whole the view of the divine Causality taken in this Lecture,
may be mentioned Lotze, the 9th Book of whose *Microcosmus*
(translated by Miss Elizabeth Hamilton and Miss Constance
Jones) or the third Book of his *Logic* (translation ed. by
Prof. Bosanquet), may very well be read by themselves
(his views may also be studied in his short *Philosophy
of Religion*—two translations, by the late Mrs. Conybeare
and by Professor Ladd) ; Pfleiderer, *Philosophy and Development of Religion*, especially chapter v. ; and Professor Ward's
Naturalism and Agnosticism.

Among the non-idealistic writers who have based their
argument for the existence of God mainly or largely upon the
consideration that Causality is unintelligible apart from a
rational Will, may be mentioned—among older writers Reid,
Essays on the Active Powers of Man, Essay I. (especially
chapter v.), and among more recent ones Martineau, *A Study
of Religion.*   Flint's *Theism* may be recommended as one of
the best attempts to state the theistic case with a minimum
of technical Metaphysic.

Two little books by Professor Andrew Seth (now Seth
Pringle-Pattison), though not primarily occupied with the
religious problem, may be mentioned as very useful intro-
ductions to Philosophy—*The Scottish Philosophers* and
Hegelianism and Personality.

LECTURE III

GOD AND THE MORAL CONSCIOUSNESS

A COURSE of purely metaphysical reasoning has led us up to the idea of God—that is to say, of a conscious and rational Mind and Will for which the world exists and by which that world and all other spirits are caused to exist. I have passed over a host of difficulties—the relation of God to time, the question whether or in what sense the world may be supposed to have a beginning and an end, the question of the relation in which God, the universal Mind, stands to other minds, the question of Free-will. These are difficulties which would involve elaborate metaphysical discussions : I shall return to some of them in a later lecture. It must suffice for the present to say that more than one answer to many of these questions might conceivably be given consistently with the view of the divine nature which I have contended for. All that I need insist on for my present purpose is—

(1) That God is personal in the sense that He is a

self-conscious, thinking, willing, feeling Being, distinguishable from each and all less perfect minds.

(2) That all other minds are in some sense brought into being by the divine Mind, while at the same time they have such a resemblance to, or community of nature with, their source that they may be regarded as not *mere* creations but as in some sense reproductions, more or less imperfect, of that source, approximating in various degrees to that ideal of Personality which is realised perfectly in God alone. In proportion as they approximate to that ideal, they are causes of their own actions, and can claim for themselves the kind of causality which we attribute in its perfection to God. I content myself now with claiming for the developed, rational human self a measure of freedom to the extent which I have just defined—that it is the real cause of its own actions. It is capable of self-determination. The man's actions are determined by his character. That is quite consistent with the admission that God is the ultimate cause of a self of such and such a character coming into existence at such and such a time.

(3) I will not say that the conception of those who regard the human mind as literally a part of the divine, so that the human consciousness is in no sense outside of the divine, is necessarily, for those who hold it, inconsistent with the conception of

personality both in God and man : I will only say
that I do not myself understand such an assertion.
I regard the human mind as derived from God, but
not as being part of God. Further discussion of
this question I reserve for my next lecture.

We have led up to the idea of God's existence.
But so far we have discovered nothing at all about
His character or purposes. And it is clear that
without some such knowledge the belief in God
could be of little or no value from any religious or
moral point of view. How are we to learn anything
about the character of God ? I imagine that at the
present day few people will attempt to prove the
goodness or benevolence of God from an empirical
examination of the facts of Nature or of History.
There is, no doubt, much in History and in Nature to
suggest the idea of Benevolence, but there is much
to suggest a directly opposite conclusion. Few of
us at the present day are likely to be much impressed
by the argument which Paley bases upon the existence of the little apparatus in the throat by which
it is benevolently arranged that, though constantly
on the point of being choked by our food, we hardly
ever are choked. I cannot help reminding you of
the characteristic passage : ' Consider a city-feast,'
he exclaims, ' what manducation, what deglutition,
and yet not one Alderman choked in a century ! '
Such arguments look at the matter from the point

of view of the Alderman : the point of view of the
turtle and the turkey is entirely forgotten. I would
not for a moment speak disrespectfully of the argument from design. Darwinism has changed its form,
but anybody who reads Edouard von Hartmann's
Philosophy of the Unconscious is not likely to rise
from its perusal with the idea that the evidences
of design have been destroyed by Darwinism, whatever he may think of Hartmann's strange conclusion
that the design can be explained by the operation
of an *unconscious* Mind or Will. The philosophical
argument of Mr. R. B. Haldane in *The Pathway
to Reality*,[1] and the purely biological argument of
Dr. John Haldane in his two lectures on *Life and
Mechanism*, and still more recently the brilliant
and very important work of M. Bergson, *L'Évolution
Creatrice* have, as it seems to me, abundantly shown
that it is as impossible as ever it was to explain even
the growth of a plant without supposing that in it
and all organic Nature there is a striving towards
an end. But the argument from design, though it
testifies to purpose in the Universe, tells us nothing
about the nature of that purpose. Purpose is one
thing ; benevolent purpose is another. Nobody's
estimate of the comparative amount of happiness
and misery in the world is worth much ; but for my
own part, if I trusted simply to empirical evidence,

[1] See especially Book II. Lect. iii.

I should not be disposed to do more than slightly
attenuate the pessimism of the Pessimists.   At all
events, Nature is far too ' red in tooth and claw '
to permit of our basing an argument for a benevolent
deity upon a contemplation of the facts of animal
and human life.   There is but one source from
which such an idea can possibly be derived—from
the evidence of our own moral consciousness.

Our moral ideals are the work of Reason.   That
the happiness of many ought to be preferred to the
happiness of one, that pleasure is better than pain,
that goodness is of more value than pleasure, that
some pleasures are better than others—such judgements are as much the work of our own Reason,
they are as much self-evident truths, as the truth
that two and two make four, or that A cannot be
both B and not B at the same time, or that two
straight lines cannot enclose a space.   We have
every right to assume that such truths hold good
for God as well as for man.   If such Idealism as I
have endeavoured to lead you to is well founded, the
mind which knows comes from God, and therefore the
knowledge which that mind possesses must also be
taken as an imperfect or fragmentary reproduction
of God's knowledge.   And the Theist who rejects
Idealism but admits the existence of self-evident
truths will be equally justified in assuming that,
for God as well as for man, two and two must make

four. We have just as much right to assume
that our moral ideas—our ideas of value—must
come from God too. For God too, as for us, there
must exist the idea, the ultimate category of the
good; and our judgements of value—judgements
that such and such an end is good or worth striving
for—in so far as they are true judgements, must be
supposed to represent His judgements. We are
conscious, in proportion as we are rational, of
pursuing ends which we judge to be good. If such
judgements reveal God's judgements, God must be
supposed to aim likewise at an ideal of good—the
same ideal which is revealed to us by our moral
judgements. In these judgements then we have a
revelation, the only possible revelation, of the
character of God. The argument which I have
suggested is simply a somewhat exacter statement of
the popular idea that Conscience is the voice of God.

Further to vindicate the idea of the existence,
authority, objective validity of Conscience would
lead us too far away into the region of Moral Philosophy for our present subject. I will only attempt
very briefly to guard against some possible mis-
understandings, and to meet some obvious objections:

(1) It need hardly be pointed out that the assertion of the existence of the Moral Consciousness is
not in the slightest degree inconsistent with recog-
nising its gradual growth and development. The

moral faculty, like every other faculty or aspect or activity of the human soul, has grown gradually. No rational man doubts the validity—no Idealist doubts the *a priori* character—of our mathematical judgements because probably monkeys and possibly primitive men cannot count, and certainly cannot perform more than the very simplest arithmetical operations. Still less do we doubt the validity of mathematical reasoning because not only children and savages, but sometimes even distinguished classical scholars—a Macaulay, a Matthew Arnold, a T. S. Evans,—were wholly incapable of understanding very simple mathematical arguments. Equally little do we deny a real difference between harmony and discord because people may be found who see no difference between ' God save the King ' and ' Pop goes the Weasel.' Self-evident truth does not mean truth which is evident to everybody.

(2) It is not doubted that the gradual evolution of our actual moral ideas—our actual ideas about what is right or wrong in particular cases — has been largely influenced by education, environment, association, social pressure, superstition, perhaps natural selection—in short, all the agencies by which naturalistic Moralists try to account for the existence of Morality. Even Euclid, or whatever his modern substitute may be, has to be taught; but that does not show that Geometry is an arbitrary system

invented by the ingenious and interested devices
of those who want to get money by teaching it.
Arithmetic was invented largely as an instrument
of commerce ; but it could not have been invented
if there were really no such things as number and
quantity, or if the human mind had no original
capacity for recognizing them.   Our scientific ideas,
our political ideas, our ideas upon a thousand
subjects have been partly developed, partly thwarted
and distorted in their growth, by similar influences.
But, however great the difficulty of getting rid of
these distorting influences and facing such questions
in a perfectly dry light, nobody suggests that objective truth on such matters is non-existent or for
ever unattainable.   A claim for objective validity
for the moral judgement does not mean a claim for
infallibility on behalf of any individual Conscience.
We may make mistakes in Morals just as we may
make mistakes in Science, or even in pure Mathe-
matics.   If a class of forty small boys are asked to
do a sum, they will probably not all bring out the same
answer : but nobody doubts that one answer alone
is right, though arithmetical capacity is a variable
quantity.   What is meant is merely that, if I am
right in affirming that this is good, you cannot be
likewise right in saying that it is bad : and that
we have some capacity—though doubtless a
variable capacity—of judging which is the true

view. Hence our moral judgements, in so far as
they are true judgements, must be taken to be reproductions in us of the thought of God. To show that
an idea has been gradually developed, tells us nothing
as to its truth or falsehood—one way or the other.

(3) In comparing the self-evidence of moral to
that of mathematical judgements, it is not suggested
that our moral judgements in detail are as certain,
as clear and sharply defined, as mathematical
judgements, or that they can claim so universal a con-
sensus among the competent. What is meant is
merely (a) that the notion of good in general is an
ultimate category of thought; that it contains a
meaning intelligible not perhaps to every individual
human soul, but to the normal, developed, human
consciousness; and (b) that the ultimate truth of
morals, if it is seen at all, must be seen immediately.
An ultimate moral truth cannot be deduced from,
or proved by, any other truth. You cannot prove
that pleasure is better than pain, or that virtue is
better than pleasure, to any one who judges differently.
It does not follow that all men have an equally clear
and delicate moral consciousness. The power of
discriminating moral values differs as widely as the
power of distinguishing musical sounds, or of ap-
preciating what is excellent in music. Some men
may be almost or altogether without such a power
of moral discrimination, just as some men are wholly

destitute of an ear for music ; while the higher
degrees of moral appreciation are the possession of
the few rather than of the many. Moral insight is
not possessed by all men in equal measure. Moral
genius is as rare as any other kind of genius.

(4) When we attribute Morality to God, it is not
meant that the conduct which is right for men in
detail ought to be or could possibly in all cases be
practised by God. It is a childish objection (though
it is sometimes made by modern philosophers who
should know better) to allege with Aristotle that
God cannot be supposed to make or keep contracts.
And in the same way, when we claim universal
validity for our moral judgements, we do not mean
that the rules suitable for human conduct would be
the same for beings differently organized and constituted. Our rules of sexual Morality are clearly
applicable only to sexually constituted beings.
What is meant in asserting that these rules are
universally and objectively valid is that these are
the rules which every rational intelligence, in proportion as it is rational, will recognize as being
suitable, or conducive to the ideal life, in beings
constituted as we are. The truth that permanent
monogamous marriage represents the true type of
sexual relations for human beings will be none the
less an objectively valid ethical truth, because the
lower animals are below it, while superior beings,

it may be, are above it. Universal love is none the
less the absolute moral ideal because it would be
absurd to say that beasts of prey do wrong in devour-
ing other creatures, or because war is sometimes
necessary as a means to the end of love at our present
imperfect stage of social and intellectual development. The means to the highest good vary with
circumstances ; the amount of good that is attainable
in such and such circumstances varies also ; consequently the right course of conduct will be different
for beings differently constituted or placed under
different circumstances : but the principles which,
in the view of a perfect intelligence, would determine
what is the right course for different beings in
different circumstances will be always the same.
The ultimate principles of our moral judgement,
e.g. that love is better than hate, are just as applicable to God as they are to us. Our conception
of the highest good may be inadequate ; but we
certainly shall not attain to greater adequacy, or a
nearer approach to ultimate truth, by flatly con-
tradicting our own moral judgements. It would be
just as reasonable to argue that because the law of
gravitation might be proved, from the point of view
of the highest knowledge, to be an inadequate statement of the truth, and all inadequacy involves some
error, therefore we had better assume that from the
point of view of God there is no difference whatever

between attraction and repulsion. All arguments
for what is called a ' super-moral ' Deity or a ' super-
moral ' Absolute are open to this fatal objection :
moral judgements cannot possibly rest upon anything
but the moral consciousness, and yet these doctrines
contradict the moral consciousness. The idea of
good is derived from the moral consciousness. When
a man declares that from the point of view of the
Universe all things are very good, he gets the idea
of good from his own moral consciousness, and is
assuming the objective validity of its dictates.
His judgement is an ethical judgement as much as
mine when I say that to me some things in this
world appear very bad. If he is not entitled to
assume the validity of his ethical judgements, his
proposition is false or meaningless. If he is entitled
to assume their validity, why should he distrust
that same moral consciousness when it affirms (as
it undoubtedly does) that pain and sin are for ever
bad, and not (as our ' super-moral ' Religionists
suggest) additional artistic touches which only add
to the æsthetic effect of the whole ?

I shall now proceed to develope some of the consequences which (as it appears to me) flow from the
doctrine that our belief in the goodness of God is an
inference from our own moral consciousness :

(1) It throws light on the relations between
Religion and Morality. The champions of ethical

education as a substitute for Religion and of ethical
societies as a substitute for Churches are fond of
assuming that Religion is not only unnecessary to,
but actually destructive of, the intrinsic authority
of the moral law. If we supposed with a few theologians in the most degenerate periods of Theology
(with William of Occam, some extreme Calvinists,
and a few eighteenth - century divines like Arch-
deacon Paley) that actions are right or wrong merely
because willed by God—meaning by God simply a
powerful being without goodness or moral character,
then undoubtedly the Secularists would be right.
If a religious Morality implies that Virtue means
merely (in Paley's words) ' the doing good to mankind in obedience to the will of God and for the sake
of everlasting happiness ' (so that if God were to will
murder and adultery, those practices would forth-
with become meritorious), then undoubtedly it
would be better to teach Morality without Religion
than with it. But that is a caricature of the true
teaching of Christ or of any considerable Christian
theologian. Undoubtedly we must assert what is
called the ' independence ' of the moral judgement.
The judgement ' to love is better than to hate ' has
a meaning complete in itself, which contains no reference whatever to any theological presupposition.
It is a judgement which is, and which can intelligibly
be, made by people of all religions or of none.   But

we may still raise the question whether the validity
of that judgement can be defended without theological
implications. And I am prepared most distinctly
to maintain that it cannot. These moral judgements
claim objective validity. When we say 'this is
right,' we do not mean merely 'I approve this course
of conduct,' 'this conduct gives me a thrill of satisfaction, a "feeling of approbation," a pleasure of
the moral sense.' If that were all that was meant,
it would be perfectly possible that another person
might feel an equally satisfactory glow of approbation at conduct of a precisely opposite character
without either of them being wrong. A bull-fight
fills most Spaniards with feelings of lively approbation, and most Englishmen with feelings of acute
disapprobation. If such moral judgements were mere
feelings, neither of them would be wrong. There
could be no question of objective rightness or wrong-
ness. Mustard is not objectively nice or objectively
nasty : it is simply nice to some people and nasty
to others. The mustard-lover has no right to condemn the mustard-hater, or the mustard-hater the
mustard-lover. If Morality were merely a matter
of feeling or emotion, actions would not be objectively
right or objectively wrong ; but simply right to
some people, wrong to others. Hume would be
right in holding the morality of an action to consist
simply in the pleasure it gives to the person who

contemplates it. Rightness thus becomes simply a
name for the fact of social approbation.[1] And yet
surely the very heart of the affirmation which the
moral consciousness makes in each of us is that right
and wrong are not matters of mere subjective feeling.
When I assert ' this is right,' I do not claim personal
infallibility. I may, indeed, be wrong, as I may be
wrong in my political or scientific theories. But I
do mean that I think I am right ; and that, if I am
right, you cannot also be right when you affirm that
this same action is wrong. This objective validity
is the very core and centre of the idea of Duty or
moral obligation. That is why it is so important
to assert that moral judgements are the work of
Reason, not of a supposed moral sense or any other
kind of feeling. Feelings may vary in different men
without any of them being in the wrong ; red really
is the same as green to a colour-blind person. What
we mean when we talk about the existence of Duty
is that things are right or wrong, no matter what
you or I think about them—that the laws of Morality

---

[1] ' We do not infer a character to be virtuous, because it pleases :
but in feeling that it pleases after such a particular manner, we in
effect feel that it is virtuous.' (*Treatise*, Part I. § ii., ed. Green and
Grose, vol. ii. p. 247.) ' The distinction of moral good and evil is
founded in the pleasure or pain, which results from the view of any
sentiment, or character ; and as that pleasure or pain cannot be
unknown to the person who feels it, it follows that there is just so much
virtue in any character as every one places in it, and that 'tis impossible
in this particular we can ever be mistaken.' (*Ibid.* vol. ii. p. 311.)

are quite as much independent of my personal likings
and dislikings as the physical laws of Nature.   That
is what is meant by the ' objectivity ' of the moral
law.

Now, the question arises—' Can such an objectivity be asserted by those who take a purely materialistic or naturalistic view of the Universe ? '   Whatever our metaphysical theories about the nature of
Reality may be, we can in practice have no difficulty
in the region of Physical Science about recognizing
an objective reality of some kind which is other
than my mere thinking about it.   That fire will burn
whether I think so or not is practically recognized
by persons of all metaphysical persuasions.   If I
say ' I can cloy the hungry edge of appetite by bare
imagination of a feast,' I try the experiment, and I
fail.   I imagine the feast, but I am hungry still :
and if I persist in the experiment, I die.   But what do
we mean when we say that things are right or wrong
whether I think them so or not, that the Moral Law
exists outside me and independently of my thinking
about it ?   Where and how does this moral law exist ?
The physical laws of Nature may be supposed by
the Materialist or the Realist somehow to exist
in matter : to the Metaphysician there may be difficulties in such a view, but the difficulties are not
obvious to common-sense.   But surely (whatever
may be thought about physical laws) the moral law,

which expresses not any matter of physical fact but what *ought* to be thought of acts, cannot be supposed to exist in a purely material Universe. An ' ought ' can exist only in and for a mind. In what mind, then, does the moral law exist ? As a matter of fact, different people's moral judgements contradict one another. And the consciousness of no living man can well be supposed to be a flawless reflection of the absolute moral ideal. On a non-theistic view of the Universe, then, the moral law cannot well be thought of as having any actual existence. The objective validity of the moral law can indeed be and no doubt is *asserted*, believed in, acted upon without reference to any theological creed ; but it cannot be defended or fully justified without the presupposition of Theism. What we mean by an objective law is that the moral law is a part of the ultimate nature of things, on a level with the laws of physical nature, and it cannot be *that*, unless we assume that law to be an expression of the same mind in which physical laws originate. The idea of duty, when analysed, implies the idea of God. Whatever else Plato meant by the ' idea of the good,' this at least was one of his meanings—that the moral law has its source in the source of all Reality.

And therefore at bottom popular feeling is right in holding that religious belief is necessary to Morality. Of course I do not mean to say that, were

religious belief to disappear from the world, Morality
would disappear too. But I do think Morality would
become quite a different thing from what it has been
for the higher levels of religious thought and feeling.
The best men would no doubt go on acting up to
their own highest ideal just as if it did possess
objective validity, no matter how unable they might
be to reconcile their practical with their speculative
beliefs. But it would not be so for the many—or
perhaps even for the few in their moments of weak-
ness and temptation, when once the consequences
of purely naturalistic Ethics were thoroughly admitted and realized. The only kind of objective
validity which can be recognized on a purely naturalistic view of Ethics is conformity to public opinion.
The tendency of all naturalistic Ethics is to make a
God of public opinion. And if no other deity were
recognized, such a God would assuredly not be without worshippers. And yet the strongest temptation
to most of us is the temptation to follow a debased
public opinion—the opinion of our age, our class,
our party. Apart from faith in a perfectly righteous
God whose commands are, however imperfectly,
revealed in the individual Conscience, we can find
no really valid reason why the individual should act
on his own sense of what is intrinsically right, even
when he finds himself an 'Athanasius contra mundum,'
and when his own personal likings and inclinations

and interests are on the side of the world. Kant
was at bottom right, though perhaps he did not
give the strongest reasons for his position, in making
the idea of God a postulate of Morality.

From a more directly practical point of view I
need hardly point out how much easier it is to feel
towards the moral law the reverence that we ought
to feel when we believe that that law is embodied
in a personal Will. Not only is religious Morality
not opposed to the idea of duty for duty's sake :
it is speculatively the only reasonable basis of it;
practically and emotionally the great safeguard of
it. And whatever may be thought of the possibility
of a speculative defence of such an idea without
Theism, the practical difficulty of teaching it—
especially to children, uneducated and unreflective
persons—seems to be quite insuperable.[1] In more
than one country in which religious education has
been banished from the primary schools, grave
observers complain that the idea of Duty seems to
be suffering an eclipse in the minds of the rising genera-

[1] There are no doubt ways of making Morality the law of the
Universe without what most of us understand by Theism, though
not without Religion, and a Religion of a highly metaphysical
character ; but because such non-theistic modes of religious thought
exist in Buddhism, for instance, it does not follow that they are
reasonable, and, at all events, they are hardly intelligible to most
Western minds. Such non-theistic Religions imply a Metaphysic quite as much as Christianity or Buddhism. There have been
Religions without the idea of a personal God, but never without
Metaphysic, *i.e.* a theory about the ultimate nature of things.

tion; some of them add that in those lands crime is steadily on the increase. Catechisms of civil duty and the like have not hitherto proved very satisfactory substitutes for the old teaching about the fear of God. Would that it were more frequently remembered on both sides of our educational squabbles that the supreme object of all religious education should be to instil into children's minds in the closest possible connexion the twin ideas of God and of Duty !

(2) I have tried to show that the ethical importance of the idea of God is prior to and independent of any belief in the idea of future rewards and punishments or of a future life, however conceived of. But when the idea of a righteous God has once been accepted, the idea of Immortality seems to me to follow from it as a sort of corollary. If any one on a calm review of the actual facts of the world's history can suppose that such a world as ours could be the expression of the will of a rational and moral Being without the assumption of a future life for which this is a discipline or education or preparatory stage, argument would be useless with him. Inveterate Optimism, like inveterate Scepticism, admits of no refutation, but in most minds produces no conviction. For those who are convinced that the world has a rational end, and yet that life as we see it (taken by itself) cannot be that end, the hypothesis

of Immortality becomes a necessary deduction from
their belief in God.

I would not disparage the educative effect of the
belief in a future life even when expressed in the
crude and inadequate metaphor of reward and
punishment. Few of us, I venture to think, have
reached the moral level at which the belief—not in
a vindictive, retributive, unending torment, but
in a disciplinary or purgatorial education of souls
prolonged after death—is without its value. At
the same time it is a mere caricature of all higher
religious beliefs when the religious motive is supposed to mean simply a fear of punishment and hope
of personal reward, even of the least sensuous or
material kind. Love of goodness for its own sake
is for the Theist identical with the love of God.
Love of a Person is a stronger force than devotion
to an idea ; and an ethical conception of God carries
with it the idea of Immortality.

> The wages of sin is death : if the wages of Virtue be dust,
>   Would she have heart to endure for the life of the worm
>   and the fly ?
> She desires no isles of the blest, no quiet seats of the just,
>   To rest in a golden grove, or to bask in a summer sky :
> Give her the wages of going on, and not to die.[1]

Belief in human Immortality is, as I have suggested,
the postulate without which most of us cannot

1 Tennyson's *Wages*.

believe in God. Even for its own sake it is of the
highest ethical value. The belief in Immortality gives
a meaning to life even when it has lost all other
meaning. 'It is rather,' in the noble words of the
late Professor Sidgwick, ' from a disinterested aver-
sion to an universe so irrationally constituted that
the wages of virtue should be dust than from any
private reckoning about his own wages,' that the
good man clings to the idea of Immortality. And
that is not all. The value of all higher goods even
in this life, though it does not depend wholly upon
their duration, does partly depend upon it. It
would be better to be pure and unselfish for a day
than to be base and selfish for a century. And yet
we do not hesitate to commend the value of intellectual and of all kinds of higher enjoyments on
account of their greater durability. Why, then,
should we shrink from admitting that the value of
character really is increased when it is regarded as
surviving bodily death ? Disbelief in Immortality
would, I believe, in the long run and for the vast
majority of men, carry with it an enormous enhance-
ment of the value of the carnal and sensual over the
spiritual and intellectual element in life.

(3) A third consequence which follows from our
determining to accept the moral consciousness as
containing the supreme revelation of God is this.
From the point of view of the moral consciousness

we cannot say that the Universe is wholly good.
We have only one means of judging whether things
are good or bad : the idea of value is wholly derived
from our own ethical judgements or judgements of
value. If we distrust these judgements, there is no
higher court to which we can appeal. And if we
distrust our most ultimate judgements of value, I
do not know why we should trust any judgements
whatever. Even if we grant that from some very
transcendental metaphysical height—the height, for
instance, of Mr. Bradley's Philosophy—it may be
contended that none of our judgements are wholly
true or fully adequate to express the true nature of
Reality, *we* at all events cannot get nearer to Reality
than we are conducted by the judgements which
present themselves to us as immediate and self-
evident. Now, if we do apply these judgements of
value to the Universe as we know it, can we say that
everything in it seems to be very good ? For my
own part, I unhesitatingly say, ' Pain is an evil,
and sin is a worse evil, and nothing on earth can
ever make them good.' How then are we to account
for such evils in a Universe which we believe to express the thought and will of a perfectly righteous
Being ? In only one way that I know of—by
supposing they are means to a greater good. That
is really the substance and substratum of all the
Theodicies of all the Philosophers and all the Theo-

logians except those who frankly trample on or throw over the Moral Consciousness, and declare that, for those who see truly, pain and sin are only additional sources of æsthetic interest in a great world-drama produced for his own entertainment by a Deity not anthropomorphic enough to love but still anthropomorphic enough to be amused.

I shall be told no doubt that this is limiting God. A human being may, it will be urged, without loss of goodness, do things in themselves evil, as a means to a greater good : as a surgeon, he may cause excruciating pain ; as a statesman or a soldier, he may doom thousands to a cruel death ; as a wise administrator of the poor law, he may refuse to relieve much suffering, in order that he may not cause more suffering.   But this is because his power is limited ; he has to work upon a world which has a nature of its own independent of his volition.   To apply the same explanation to the evil which God causes, is to make Him finite instead of Infinite, limited in power instead of Omnipotent.   Now in a sense I admit that this is so.   I am not wedded to the words ' Infinite ' or ' Omnipotent.'   But I would protest against a persistent misrepresentation of the point of view which I defend.   It is suggested that the limit to the power of God must necessarily spring from the existence of some other thing or being outside of Him, not created by Him or under His control. I must protest that that is not so. Everybody admits that God cannot change the past ; few Philosophers consider it necessary to maintain that God could construct triangles with their angles not together equal to two right angles, or think it any derogation from his Omnipotence to say that He could not make the sum of two and two to be other than four. Few Theologians push their idea of Freewill so far as to insist that God could will Himself to be unjust or unloving, or that, being just and loving, he could do unjust or unloving acts. There are necessities to which even God must submit. But they are not imposed upon Him from without : they are parts of His own essential nature. The limitation by which God cannot attain His ends without causing some evil is a limitation of exactly the same nature. If you say that it is no limitation of God not to be able to change the past, for the thing is really unmeaning, then I submit that in the same way it may be no limitation that He should not be able to evolve highly organized beings without a struggle for existence, or to train human beings in unselfishness without allowing the existence both of sin and of pain. From the point of view of perfect knowledge, these things might turn out to be just as unmeaning as for God to change the past. The popular idea of Omnipotence is one which really does not bear looking into. If we supposed the world to contain no evil at all, still there would be in it a definite amount of good. Twice such a world would be twice as good. Why is there not twice that amount of good ? A being who deliberately created only a good world of limited quantity—a definite number of spirits (for instance) enjoying so much pleasure and so much virtue—when he could have created twice that number of spirits, and consequently twice that amount of good, would not be perfectly good or loving. And so on *ad infinitum*, no matter how much good you suppose him to have created. The only sense which we can intelligibly give to the idea of a divine Omnipotence is this— that God possesses all the power there is, that He can do all things that are in their own nature possible.[1]

But there is a more formidable objection which I have yet to meet. It has been urged by certain Philosophers of great eminence that, if we suppose God not to be unlimited in power, we have no guarantee that the world is even good on the whole ; we should not be authorized to infer anything as to a future life or the ultimate destiny of Humanity from the fact of God's goodness. A limited God might be a defeated God. I admit the difficulty. This is the 'greatest wave' of all in the theistic

---

[1] The doctrine of St. Thomas Aquinas is ' Cum possit Deus omnia efficere quæ esse possunt, non autem quæ contradictionem implicant, omnipotens merito dicitur.' (*Summa Theol.*, Pars I. Q. xxv. art. 3.)

argument. In reply, I would simply appeal to the
reasons which I have given for supposing that the
world is really willed by God. A rational being
does not will evil except as a means to a greater
good. If God be rational, we have a right to suppose
that the world must contain more good than evil,
or it would not be willed at all. A being who was
obliged to create a world which did not seem to him
good would be a blind force, as force is understood
by the pure Materialist, not a rational Will. That
much we have a right to claim as a matter of strict
Logic ; and that would to my own mind be a sufficient
reason for assuming that, at least for the higher
order of spirits, such a life as ours must be intended
as the preface to a better life than this. But I
should go further. To me it appears that such
evils as sin and pain are so enormously worse than
the mere absence of good, that I could not regard
as rational a Universe in which the good did not very
greatly predominate over the evil. More than that
I do not think we are entitled to say. And yet
Justice is so great a good that it is rational to hope
that for every individual conscious being—at least
each individual capable of any high degree of good
—there must be a predominance of good on the
whole. Beings of very small capacity might conceivably be created chiefly or entirely as a means
to a vastly greater good than any that they them-

selves enjoy : the higher a spirit is in the scale of
being, the more difficult it becomes to suppose
that it has been brought into existence merely as
a means to another's good, or that it will not ultimately enjoy a good which will make it on the whole
good that it should have been born.

I could wish myself that, in popular religious
teaching, there was a franker conception of this
position—a position which, as I have said, is
really implied in the Theodicies of all the Divines.
Popular unbelief—and sometimes the unbelief of
more cultivated persons—rests mainly upon the
existence of evil. We should cut at the roots of it
by teaching frankly that this is the best of all possible
Universes, though not the best of all imaginable
Universes—such Universes as we can construct in
our own imagination by picturing to ourselves all
the good that there is in the world without any of
the evil. We may still say, if we please, that God
is infinite because He is limited by nothing outside
His own nature, except what He has Himself caused.
We can still call Him Omnipotent in the sense that
He possesses all the power there is. And in many
ways such a belief is far more practically consolatory
and stimulating than a belief in a God who can
do all things by any means and who consequently
does not need our help. In our view, we are engaged
not in a sham warfare with an evil that is really

good, but in a real warfare with a real evil, a
struggle in which we have the ultimate power in the
Universe on our side, but one in which the victory
cannot be won without our help, a real struggle in
which we are called upon to be literally fellow-
workers with God.

LITERATURE

The subject is more or less explicitly dealt with in most
of the works mentioned at the end of the last two lectures, and
also in books on Moral Philosophy too numerous to mention.
Classical vindications of the authority of the Moral Consciousness are Bishop Butler's *Sermons*, and Kant's *Fundamental
Principles of the Metaphysic of Morals* and other ethical
writings (translated by T. K. Abbott). I have expressed my
own views on the subject with some fullness in the third
book of my *Theory of Good and Evil*.

LECTURE IV

DIFFICULTIES AND OBJECTIONS

IN the present lecture I shall try to deal with some
of the difficulties which will probably have been
arising in your minds in the course of the last three ;
and in meeting them, to clear up to some extent
various points which have been left obscure.

(1) *Creation.* I have endeavoured to show that
the world must be thought of as ultimately an
experience in the mind of God, parts of which are
progressively communicated to lesser minds such as
ours. This experience—both the complete experience which is in His own mind and also the measure
of it which is communicated to the lesser minds—
must be thought of as willed by God. At the same
time I suggested as an alternative view that, even
if we think of things as having an existence which
is not simply in and for minds, the things must be
caused to exist by a rational Will.   Now the world,
as we know it, consists of a number of changes taking
place in time, changes which are undoubtedly represented in thought as changes happening to, or acci-

dents of, a permanent substance, whether (with the
Idealist) we suppose that this substance is merely
the object of Mind's contemplation, or whether (with
the Realist) we think of it as having some sort of
being independent of Mind.   But what of the first
of these events—the beginning of the whole series ?
Are we to think of the series of events in time as
having a beginning and possibly an end, or as being
without beginning or end ?   What in fact are we
to make of the theological idea of Creation, often
further defined as Creation out of nothing ?   It is
often suggested both by Idealists and by Realists
that the idea of a creation or absolute beginning of
the world is unthinkable.   Such a view seems to me
to be a piece of unwarrantable *a priori* dogmatism—
quite as much so as the closely connected idea that
the Uniformity of Nature is an *a priori* necessity
of thought.   No doubt the notion of an absolute
beginning of all things is unthinkable enough : if
we think of God as creating the world at a definite
point of time, then we must suppose God Himself
to have existed before that creation.   We cannot
think of an event in time without thinking of a time
before it ; and time cannot be thought of as merely
empty time.   Events of some kind there must necessarily have been, even though those events are
thought of as merely subjective experiences involving
no relation to space.   A beginning of existence is,

indeed, unthinkable. But there is no difficulty in
supposing that this particular series of phenomena
which constitutes our physical Universe may have
had a beginning in time. On the other hand there
is no positive evidence, for those who cannot regard
the early chapters of Genesis as representing on such
a matter anything but a primitive legend edited by
a later Jewish thinker, that it had such a beginning.
It is no doubt more difficult to represent to ourselves
a beginning of space ; and the notion of an empty
space, eternally thought but not eternally filled up
by any series of phenomena of the space-occupying
kind, represents a rather difficult, though not (as it
seems to me) an absolutely impossible conception.
The question, therefore, whether there was a beginning of the series of events which constitute the
history of our physical world must (so far as I can
see) be left an open one.

Of course if the argument of Lord Kelvin be
accepted, if he is justified in arguing on purely
physical grounds that the present distribution of
energy in the Universe is such that it cannot have
resulted from an infinite series of previous physical
changes, if Science can prove that the series is a
finite one, the conclusions of Science must be accepted.[1] Metaphysic has nothing to say for or against
such a view. That is a question of Physics on which

[1] Cf. Flint's *Theism*, Ed. v., p. 117 and App. xi.

of course I do not venture to express any opinion whatever.

(2) *The time-series.* I am incompetent to pronounce an opinion on the validity of such arguments as Lord Kelvin's. But, however we decide this question, there will still remain the further and harder question, 'Is the series of all events or experiences, physical or psychical (not merely the particular series which constitutes our physical Universe), to be thought of as finite or infinite ? On the one hand it involves a contradiction to talk of a time-series which has a beginning : a time which has no time before it is not time at all ; any more than space with an end to it would be space. On the other hand, we find equally, or almost equally, unthinkable the hypothesis of an endless series of events in time : a series of events, which no possible enumeration of its members will make any smaller, presents itself to us as unthinkable, directly we regard it as expressing the true nature of a positive reality, and not as a mere result of mathematical abstraction.   Here then we are presented with an antinomy—an apparent contradiction in our thought —which we can neither avoid nor overcome.   It is one of the classical antinomies recognized by the Kantian Philosophy—the only one, I may add, which neither Kant himself nor any of his successors has done anything to attenuate or to remove.

Kant's own attempted solution of it involved the impossible supposition that the past has no existence at all except in so far as it is thought by some finite mind in the present. The way out of this difficulty which is popular with post-Kantian Idealists is to say that God is Himself out of time, and eternally sees the whole series at once. But, in the first place, that does not get over the difficulty : even if God does see the whole series at once, He must see it either as limited or as endless, and the old antinomy breaks out again when we attempt to think either alternative. And secondly, when you treat a temporal series as one which is all really present together—of course it may all be *known* together as even *we* know the past and the future—but when you try to think of God as contemplating the whole series as really present altogether, the series is no longer a time-series. You have turned it into some other kind of series—practically (we may say) into a spacial series. You have cut the knot, instead of unravelling it. I have no doubt that the existence of this antinomy does point to the fact that there is some way of thinking about time from which the difficulty disappears : but we are, so far as I can see, incompetent so to resolve it. Philosophers resent the idea of an insoluble problem. By all means let them go on trying to solve it. I can only say that I find no difficulty in showing the futility

of any solution of the time-difficulty which I have
so far seen. For the present at least—I strongly
suspect for ever—we must acquiesce on this matter
in a reverent Agnosticism. We can show the
absurdity of regarding time as merely subjective;
we can show that it belongs to the very essence of
the Universe we know; we can show that it is as
'objective' as anything else within our knowledge.
But how to reconcile this objectivity with the
difficulty of thinking of an endless succession no
Philosopher has done much to explain. For religious
purposes it seems enough to believe that each
member of the time-series—no matter how many
such events there may be, no matter whether the
series be endless or not—is caused by God. The
more reflecting Theologians have generally admitted
that the act of divine Conservation is essentially the
same as that of Creation. A God who can be represented as 'upholding all things by the power of his
word' is a creative Deity whether the act of creation
be in time, or eternally continuous, or (if there were
any meaning in that phrase) out of time altogether.[1]

[1] The most illuminating discussion of time and the most convincing
argument for its 'objectivity' which I know, is to be found in Lotze's
Metaphysic, Book II. chap. iii., but it cannot be recommended to
the beginner in Metaphysic. A brilliant exposition of the view of
the Universe which regards time and change as belonging to the
very reality of the Universe, has recently appeared in M. Bergson's
L'Evolution Créatrice, but he has hardly attempted to deal with
the metaphysical difficulties indicated above. The book, however,

(3) *The creation of spirits.* It may seem to some of you that I may have so far left out, or too easily disposed of, an important link in our argument. I have given reasons for thinking that the material world cannot be explained without the assumption of a universal Consciousness which both thinks and wills it. I have assumed rather than proved that the lesser minds, in which the divine experience is partially reproduced, are also caused to exist and kept in existence by the same divine Will. But how, it may be said, do we know that those minds did not exist before the birth of the organisms with which upon this planet they are connected? The considerations which forbid our thinking of matter as something capable of existing by itself do not apply to minds. A consciousness, unlike a thing, exists ' for itself,' not merely ' for another ' : a mind is not made what it is by being known or otherwise experienced by another mind : its very being consists in being itself conscious : it is what it is for itself. It is undoubtedly impossible positively to disprove the hypothesis of eternally pre-existent souls. Sometimes that hypothesis is combined with Theism. It

seems to me the most important philosophical work that has appeared since Mr. Bradley's *Appearance and Reality*, and though the writer has hardly formulated his Natural Theology, it constitutes a very important contribution to the theistic argument. Being based upon a profound study of biological Evolution, it may be specially commended to scientific readers.

is supposed that God is the supreme and incomparably the most powerful, but not the only, self-
existent and eternal Spirit.   This hypothesis—sometimes spoken of as Pluralism [1]—has many attrac-
tions : from the time of Origen onwards the idea of
Pre-existence has seemed to many to facilitate the
explanation of evil by making it possible to regard
the sufferings of our present state as a disciplinary
process for getting rid of an original or a pre-natal
sinfulness.   It is a theory not incapable of satisfying
the demands of the religious Consciousness, and may
even form an element in an essentially Christian
theory of the Universe : but to my mind it is opposed
to all the obvious indications of experience.   The
connexion between soul and body is such that the
laws of the soul's development obviously form part
of the same system with the laws of physical nature.
If one part of that system is referred to the divine
Will, so must the whole of it be.   The souls, when
they have entered animal bodies, must be supposed
to be subject to a system of laws which is of one piece
with the system of physical laws.   If the physical
part of the world-order is referred to the divine Will,
the psychical part of it must be equally referred to

[1] Such a view is expounded in Dr. Schiller's early work *The Riddles
of the Sphinx* and in Professor Howison's *The Limits of Evolution*.
The very distinguished French thinker Charles Renouvier (*La Nouvelle
Monadologie*, etc.), like Origen, believed that souls were pre-existent
but created.

that Will. The souls might, indeed, conceivably have an independent and original nature of their own capable of offering resistance to the divine intentions. But we see, to say the least, no indications of a struggle going on between an outside divine Will and independent beings not forming a part of the divine scheme. At all events, the result of this struggle, if struggle there be, is (so far as we can observe) a system, complete and orderly, within the psychical sphere as much as within the purely physical sphere. And in particular the body is exactly fitted to the soul that is to inhabit it. We never find the intellect of a Shakespeare in connexion with the facial angle of a negro ; bodies which resemble the bodies of their parents are connected with souls between which a similar resemblance can be traced. If the souls existed before birth, we must suppose those souls to be kept waiting in a limbo of some kind till a body is prepared suitable for their reception. We must suppose that among the waiting souls, one is from time to time selected to be the offspring of such and such a matrimonial union, so as to present (as it were) a colourable appearance of being really the fruit of that union. Further, before birth the souls must be steeped in the waters of Lethe, or something of the kind, so as to rid them of all memory of their previous experiences. Such a conception seems to

me to belong to the region of Mythology rather
than of sober philosophical thought. I do not
deny that Mythology may sometimes be a means
of pictorially or symbolically envisaging truths to
which Philosophy vaguely points but which it
cannot express in clearly apprehensible detail.
But such a Mythology as this seems to be intellectually unmotived and unhelpful. It is not wanted to
explain the facts : there is nothing in our experience
to suggest it, and much which is *prima facie* opposed
to it. It really removes no single difficulty : for
one difficulty which it presents some appearance of
removing, it creates a dozen greater ones. It is a
hypothesis which we shall do well to dismiss as
otiose.

(4) *Non-theistic Idealism.* Somewhat less unmotived, if we look upon it from a merely intellectual
point of view, is the theory of pre-existent souls
without a personal God. Many, if not most, of you
probably possess more or less acquaintance with the
views of my friend, Dr. McTaggart. I cannot here
undertake a full exposition or criticism of one of the
ablest thinkers of our day—one of the very few
English thinkers who is the author of a truly original
metaphysical system. I can only touch—and that
most inadequately—upon the particular side of it
which directly bears upon our present enquiry. Dr.
McTaggart is an Idealist ; he recognizes the impos-

sibility of matter without mind. For him nothing exists but spirits, but he does not recognize the necessity for any one all-embracing or controlling Spirit : the only spirits in his Universe are limited minds like those of men and animals. He differs, then, from the Pluralist of the type just mentioned in getting rid of the hypothesis of a personal God side by side with and yet controlling the uncreated spirits. And he differs further from all Pluralists in not treating the separate spirits as so many centres of consciousness quite independent of, and possibly at war with, all the rest : the spirits form part of an ordered system : the world is a unity, though that unity is not the unity which belongs to self-consciousness. He recognizes, in the traditional language of Philosophy, an Absolute, but this Absolute is not a single spiritual Being but a Society : or, if it is to be called a single spiritual Being, it is a Being which exists or manifests itself only in a plurality of limited consciousnesses.

This scheme is, I admit, more reasonable than Pluralism. It does, nominally at least, recognize the world as an ordered system. It gets rid of the difficulty of accounting for the apparent order of the Cosmos as the result of a struggle between independent wills. It is not, upon its author's presuppositions, a gratuitous theory : for a mind which accepts Idealism and rejects Theism it is the only

intelligible alternative. But I must confess that it
seems to me open to most of the difficulties which I
have endeavoured to point out in Pluralism, and to
some others. In the first place, there is one, to my
mind, great and insuperable difficulty about it. As
an Idealist, Dr. McTaggart has to admit that the
whole physical world, in so far as it exists at all,
must exist in and for some consciousness. Now,
not only is there, according to him, no single mind
in which the system can exist as a whole, but even
all the minds together do not apparently know the
whole of it, or (so far as our knowledge goes) ever will.
The undiscovered and unknown part of the Universe
is then non-existent. And yet, be it noticed, the
known part of the world does not make a perfectly
articulated or (if you like the phrase) organic system
without the unknown part. It is only on the
assumption of relations between what we know and
what we don't know that we can regard it as an
orderly, intelligible system at all. Therefore, if
part of the system is non-existent, the whole system
—the system as a whole—must be treated as non-
existent. The world is, we are told, a system ; and
yet as a system it has (upon the hypothesis) no real
existence. The systematic whole does not exist
in matter, for to Dr. McTaggart matter is merely
the experience of Mind. What sort of existence,
then, can an undiscovered planet possess till it is

discovered ? For Dr. McTaggart has not provided
any mind or minds in and for which it is to exist.
At one time, indeed, Dr. McTaggart seemed disposed
to accept a suggestion of mine that, on his view,
each soul must be omniscient ; and to admit that,
while in its temporal aspect, each soul is limited
and fallible in its knowledge, it is at the same time
supertemporally omniscient. That is a conception
difficult beyond all the difficulties of the most
arbitrary and self-contradicting of orthodox patristic
or scholastic speculations. But, as Dr. McTaggart
does not now seem disposed to insist upon that
point, I will say no more about it except that to
my mind it is a theory which defies all intellectual
grasp. It can be stated; it cannot be thought.

Further, I would remind you, the theory is open
to all the objections which I urged against the Pre-
existence theory in its pluralistic form. I have
suggested the difficulties involved in the facts of
heredity—the difficulty of understanding how
souls whose real intellectual and moral characteristics are uncaused and eternal should be assigned
to parents so far resembling them as to lead almost
inevitably to the inference that the characteristics
of the children are to some extent causally connected
with those of the parents.[1] Now the Pluralist can

---

[1] I use the word 'causally connected' in the popular or scientific sense of
the word, to indicate merely an actually observed psycho-physical law.

at least urge that for this purpose ingenious arrange-
ments are contrived by God—by the One Spirit
whom he regards as incomparably the wisest and
most powerful in the Universe. Dr. McTaggart
recognizes no intelligence capable of grappling with
such a problem or succession of problems. But
this particular matter of the assignment of souls
to bodies is only a particular application of a wider
difficulty. Dr. McTaggart contends that the Universe constitutes not merely a physical but a moral
order. He would not deny that the Universe means
something; that the series of events tends towards
an end, an end which is also a good; that it has a
purpose and a final cause. And yet this purpose
exists in no mind whatever, and is due to no will
whatever—except to the very small extent to which
the processes of physical nature can be consciously
directed to an end by the volitions of men and
similarly limited intelligences. As a whole, the
Universe is purposed and willed by no single will or
combination of wills. I confess I do not understand
the idea of a purpose which operates, but is not the
purpose of a Mind which is also a Will. All the
considerations upon which I dwelt to show the
necessity of such a Will to account for the Universe
which we know, are so many arguments against Dr.
McTaggart's scheme. The events of Dr. McTaggart's
Universe are, upon the view of Causality which I

attempted to defend in my second lecture, uncaused events.

Nevertheless, as a Philosopher, I am deeply grateful to Dr. McTaggart. Not only does his scheme on its practical side seem to me preferable to many systems which sound more orthodox— systems of vague pantheistic Theism in which Morality is treated as mere 'appearance' and personal Immortality deliberately rejected—but it has done much intellectually to clear the air. Dr. McTaggart seems to me right in holding that, if God or the Absolute is to include in itself all other spirits, and yet the personality or self-consciousness of those spirits is not to be denied, then this Absolute in which they are to be included cannot reasonably be thought of as a conscious being, or invested with the other attributes usually implied by the term God.

And this leads me to say a few words more in explanation of my own view of the relation between God and human or other souls. To me, as I have already intimated, it seems simply meaningless to speak of one consciousness as included in another consciousness. The essence of a consciousness is to be for itself : whether it be a thought, a feeling, or an emotion, the essence of that consciousness is what it is for me. Every moment of consciousness is unique. Another being may have a

similar feeling : in that case there are two feelings,
and not one. Another mind may know what I
feel, but the knowledge of another's agony is (fortunately) a very different thing from the agony
itself. It is fashionable in some quarters to ridicule
the idea of 'impenetrable' souls. If 'impenetrable'
means that another soul cannot know what goes on
in my soul, I do not assert that the soul is impenetrable. I believe that God knows what occurs in
my soul in an infinitely completer way than that in
which any human being can know it. Further, I
believe that every soul is kept in existence from
moment to moment by a continuous act of the
divine Will, and so is altogether dependent upon
that Will, and forms part of one system with Him.
On the other hand I believe that (through the
analogy of my own mind and the guidance of the
moral consciousness) I do know, imperfectly and
inadequately, ' as in a mirror darkly,' what goes on
in God's Mind. But, if penetrability is to mean
identity, the theory that souls are penetrable seems
to me mainly unintelligible. The acceptance which
it meets with in some quarters is due, I believe,
wholly to the influence of that most fertile source
of philosophical confusion—misapplied spacial metaphor.[1] It seems easy to talk about a mind being

---

[1] In part, perhaps, also to a mistaken theory of predication, which
assumes that, because every fact in the world can be represented as

something in itself, and yet part of another mind, because we are familiar with the idea of things in space forming part of larger things in space—Chinese boxes, for instance, shut up in bigger ones. Such a mode of thought is wholly inapplicable to minds which are not in space at all. Space is in the mind : the mind is not in space. A mind is not a thing which can be round or square : you can't say that the intellect of Kant or of Lord Kelvin measures so many inches by so many : equally impossible is it to talk about such an intellect being a part of a more extensive intellect.

The theory of an all-inclusive Deity has recently been adopted and popularized by Mr. Campbell,[1] who has done all that rhetorical skill combined with genuine religious earnestness can do to present it in an attractive and edifying dress. And yet the same Logic which leads to the assertion that the Saint is part of God, leads also to the assertion that Cæsar Borgia and Napoleon Buonaparte and all the wicked Popes who have ever been white-washed by episcopal or other historians are also parts of God. How can I worship, how can I strive to be like, how can I be the better for believing in or revering

logically a predicate of Reality at large, therefore there is but one Substance or (metaphysically) Real Being in the world, of which all other existences are really mere 'attributes.' But this theory cannot be discussed here.

[1] In *The New Theology.*

a Being of whom Cæsar Borgia is a part as completely
and entirely as St. Paul or our Lord himself ?
Hindoo Theology is consistent in this matter. It
worships the destructive and the vicious aspects
of Brahma as much as the kindly and the moral
ones : it does not pretend that God is revealed in
the Moral Consciousness, or is in any exclusive or
one-sided way a God of Love. If it be an ' ethical
obsession ' (as has been suggested) to object to treat
Immorality as no less a revelation of God than
Morality, I must plead guilty to such an obsession.
And yet without such an ' obsession ' I confess I
do not see what is left of Christianity. There is
only one way out of the difficulty. If we are all
parts of God, we can only call God good or perfect
by maintaining that the deliverances of our moral
consciousness have no validity for God, and therefore can tell us nothing about him. That has been
done deliberately and explicitly by some Philosophers : [1] the distinguished Theologians who echo
the language of this Philosophy have fortunately
for their own religious life and experience, but
unfortunately for their philosophical consistency,
declined to follow in their steps. A God who is
' beyond good and evil,' can be no fitting object of

[1] *E.g.* by Mr. Bradley in *Appearance and Reality* and still more
uncompromisingly by Professor A. E. Taylor in *The Problem of
Conduct*, but I rejoice to find that the latter very able writer has
recently given up this theory of a ' super-moral' Absolute.

worship to men who wish to become good, just, merciful. If the cosmic process be indifferent to these ethical considerations, we had better (with honest Agnostics like Professor Huxley) make up our minds to defy it, whether it call itself God or not.

But it is not so much on account of its conse-quences as on account of its essential unmeaning-ness and intellectual unintelligibility that I would invite you to reject this formula ' God is all.' Cer-tainly, the Universe is an ordered system : there is nothing in it that is not done by the Will of God. And some parts of this Universe—the spiritual parts of it and particularly the higher spirits—are not mere creations of God's will. They have a resemblance of nature to Him. I do not object to your saying that at bottom there is but one Sub-stance in the Universe, if you will only keep clear of the materialistic and spacial association of the word Substance : but it is a Substance which reveals itself in many different consciousnesses. The theory of an all-inclusive Consciousness is not necessary to make possible the idea of close and intimate com-munion between God and men, or of the revelation in and to Humanity of the thought of God. On the contrary, it is the idea of Identity which destroys the possibility of communion. Communion implies two minds : a mind cannot have communion with itself or with part of itself. The two may also in a sense be one ; of course all beings are ultimately part of one Universe or Reality : but that Reality is not one Consciousness. The Universe is a unity, but the unity is not of the kind which constitutes a person or a self-consciousness. It is (as Dr. McTaggart holds) the unity of a Society, but of a Society (as I have attempted to argue) which emanates from, and is controlled by and guided to a preconceived end by, a single rational Will.[1]

(5) *The intuitive theory of religious knowledge.* In other quarters objection will probably be taken to my not having recognized the possibility of an immediate knowledge of God, and left the idea of God to be inferred by intellectual processes which, when fully thought out, amount to a Metaphysic. It will be suggested that to make religious belief dependent upon Reason is to make it impossible to any but trained Philosophers or Theologians. Now there is no doubt a great attractiveness in the theory which makes belief in God depend simply upon the immediate affirmation of the individual's own consciousness. It would be more difficult to argue against such a theory of immediate knowledge or intuition if we found that the consciousness of all or most individuals does actually reveal to them

[1] I think it desirable to mention here that Professor Watson's account of my views in his *Philosophical Basis of Religion* completely misrepresents my real position. I have replied to his criticisms in *Mind*, N.S. No. 69 (Jan. 1909).

the existence of God : though after all the fact
that a number of men draw the same inference
from given facts does not show that it is not an
inference. You will sometimes find Metaphysicians
contending that nobody is really an Atheist, since
everybody necessarily supposes himself to be in
contact with an Other of which he is nevertheless
a part. I do not deny that, if you water down the
idea of God to the notion of a vague 'something
not ourselves,' you may possibly make out that
everybody is explicitly or implicitly a believer
in such a Deity.

I should prefer myself to say that, if that is all
you mean by God, it does not much matter whether
we believe in Him or not. In the sense in which
God is understood by Christianity or Judaism or any
other theistic Religion it is unfortunately impossible
to contend that everybody is a Theist. And, if there
is an immediate knowledge of God in every human
soul, this would be difficult to account for. Neither
the cultivated nor the uncultivated Chinaman has
apparently any such belief. The ignorant Chinaman believes in a sort of luck or destiny—possibly
in a plurality of limited but more or less mischievous
spirits : the educated Chinaman, we are told, is for
the most part a pure Agnostic. And Chinamen are
believed to be one-fifth of the human race. The task
of the Missionary would be an easier one if he could

appeal to any such widely diffused intuitions of God.
The Missionary, from the days of St. Paul at Athens
down to the present, has to begin by arguing with his
opponents in favour of Theism, and then to go on to
argue from Theism to Christianity. I do not deny
—on the contrary I strongly contend—that the
rational considerations which lead up to Monotheism
are so manifold, and lie so near at hand, that at a
certain stage of mental development we find that
belief independently asserting itself with more or less
fullness in widely distant regions of time and space;
while traces of it are found almost everywhere—even
among savages—side by side with other and inconsistent beliefs. But even among theistic nations
an immediate knowledge of God is claimed by very
few. If there is a tendency on the part of the more
strongly religious minds to claim it, it is explicitly
disclaimed by others—by most of the great Schoolmen, and in modern times by profoundly religious
minds such as Newman or Martineau. Its existence
is in fact denied by most of the great theological
systems—Catholic, Protestant, Anglican. Theologians always begin by arguing in favour of the
existence of God. And even among the religious
minds without philosophical training which do claim
such immediate knowledge, their creed is most often
due (as is obvious to the outside observer) to the
influence of environment, of education, of social

tradition. For the religious person who claims such knowledge of God does not generally stop at the bare affirmation of God's existence : he goes on to claim an immediate knowledge of all sorts of other things—ideas clearly derived from the traditional teaching of his religious community. The Protestant of a certain type will claim immediate consciousness of ideas about the forgiveness of sins which are palpably due to the teaching of Luther or St. Augustine, and to the influence of this or that preacher who has transmitted those ideas to him or to his mother : while the Catholic, though his training discourages such claims, will sometimes see visions which convey to him an immediate assurance of the truth of the Immaculate Conception. Even among Anglicans we find educated men who claim to know by immediate intuition the truth of historical facts alleged to have occurred in the first century, or dogmatic truths such as the complicated niceties of the Athanasian Creed. These claims to immediate insight thus refute themselves by the inconsistent character of the knowledge claimed. An attempt may be made to extract from all these immediate certainties a residual element which is said to be common to all of them. The attempt has been made by Professor James in that rather painful work, the *Varieties of Religious Experience.* And the residuum turns out to be something so vague that, if not absolutely worthless, it is almost incapable of being expressed in articulate language, and constitutes a very precarious foundation for a working religious creed.

The truth is that the uneducated—or rather the unanalytical, perhaps I ought to say the metaphysically untrained—human mind has a tendency to regard as an immediate certainty any truth which it strongly believes and regards as very important. Such minds do not know the psychological causes which have led to their own belief, when they are due to psychological causes: they have not analysed the processes of thought by which they have been led to those beliefs which are really due to the working of their own minds. Most uncultivated persons would probably be very much surprised to hear that the existence of the friend with whose body they are in physical contact is after all only an inference.[1] But surely, in the man who has discovered that such is the case, the warmth of friendship was never dimmed by the reflection that his knowledge of his friend is not immediate but mediate. It is a mere prejudice to suppose that mediate knowledge is in any

---

[1] This is sometimes denied by Philosophers, but I have never been able to understand on what grounds. If I know *a priori* the existence of other men, I ought to be able to say *a priori* how many they are and to say something about them. And this is more than any one claims.

way less certain, less intimate, less trustworthy
or less satisfying than immediate knowledge. If
we claim for man the possibility of just such a knowledge of God as a man may possess of his brother
man, surely that is all that is wanted to make possible
the closest religious communion. It is from the
existence of my own self that I infer the existence
of other selves, whom I observe to behave in a manner
resembling my own behaviour. It is by an only
slightly more difficult and complicated inference
from my own consciousness that I rise to that
conception of a universal Consciousness which
supplies me with at once the simplest and the most
natural explanation both of my own existence and
of the existence of the Nature which I see around
me.

(6) *Religion and Psychology.* I do not deny that
the study of religious history, by exhibiting the
naturalness and universality of religious ideas and
religious emotions, may rationally create a pre-
disposition to find some measure of truth in every
form of religious belief. But 1 would venture to
add a word of caution against the tendency fashionable in many quarters to talk of basing religious
belief upon Psychology. The business of Psychology
is to tell us what actually goes on in the human mind.
It cannot possibly tell us whether the beliefs which
are found there are true or false. An erroneous

belief is as much a psychological fact as a true one.
A theory which goes on, by inference from what
we observe in our own minds, to construct a theory
of the Universe necessarily involves a Metaphysic,
conscious or unconscious. It may be urged that
the reality of religious experience is unaffected by the
question whether the beliefs associated with it are
true or false. That is the case, so long as the beliefs
are supposed to be true by the person in question.
But, when once the spirit of enquiry is aroused, a
man cannot be—and I venture to think ought not
to be—satisfied as to the truth of his belief simply
by being told that the beliefs are actually there.

It may be contended, no doubt, that religious
experience does not mean merely a state of intellectual belief, but certain emotions, aspirations,
perhaps (to take one particular type of religious
experience) a consciousness of love met by answering
love. To many who undergo such experiences,
they seem to carry with them an immediate assurance
of the existence of the Being with whom they feel
themselves to be in communion. That, on the
intellectual presuppositions of the particular person,
seems to be the natural—it may be the only possible
—way of explaining the feeling. But even there
the belief is not really immediate : it is an inference
from what is actually matter of experience. And
it is, unhappily, no less a matter of well-ascertained

psychological fact that, when intellectual doubt is once aroused, such experiences no longer carry with them this conviction of their own objective basis. The person was really under the influence of an intellectual theory all along, whether the theory was acquired by hereditary tradition, by the influence of another's mind, or by personal thought and reflection. When the intellectual theory alters, the same kind of experience is no longer possible. I will not attempt to say how far it is desirable that persons who are perfectly satisfied with a creed which they have never examined should (as it were) pull up the roots of their own faith to see how deep they go. I merely want to point out that the occurrence of certain emotional experiences, though undoubtedly they may constitute part of the data of a religious argument, cannot be held to constitute in and by themselves sufficient evidence for the truth of the intellectual theory connected with them in the mind of the person to whom they occur. They do not always present themselves as sufficient evidence for their truth even to the person experiencing them—still less can they do so to others. Equally unreasonable is it to maintain, with a certain class of religious philosophers, that the religious experience by itself is all we want ; and to assume that we may throw to the winds all the theological or other beliefs which have actually been associated with the various types of religious experience, and yet continue to have those experiences and find them no less valuable and no less satisfying. If there is one thing which the study of religious Psychology testifies to, it is the fact that the character of the religious experience (though there may be certain common elements in it) varies very widely with the character of the theoretical belief with which it is associated—a belief of which it is sometimes the cause, sometimes the effect, but from which it is always inseparable. The Buddhist's religious experiences are not possible to those who hold the Christian's view of the Universe : the Christian's religious experiences are not possible to one who holds the Buddhist theory of the Universe. You cannot have an experience of communion with a living Being when you disbelieve in the existence of such a Being. And a man's theories of the Universe always at bottom imply a Metaphysic of some kind—conscious or unconscious.

Sometimes the theory of a Religion which shall be purely psychological springs from pure ignorance as to the meaning of the terms actually employed by the general usage of philosophers. Those who talk in this way mean by Psychology what, according to the ordinary philosophic usage, is really Metaphysic. For Metaphysic is simply the science which deals with the ultimate nature of the Universe.

At other times attempts are made by people of more or less philosophical culture to justify their theory. The most widely influential of such attempts is the one made by M. Auguste Sabatier.[1] This attempt has at least this much in its favour—that it is not so much to the ordinary experience of average men and women that M. Sabatier appeals as to the exceptional experiences of the great religious minds. He lays the chief stress upon those exceptional moments of religious history when a new religious idea entered into the mind of some prophet or teacher, *e.g.* the unity of God, the Fatherhood of God, the brotherhood of Man. Here, just because the idea was new, it cannot (he contends) be accounted for by education or environment or any other of the psychological causes which obviously determine the traditional beliefs of the great majority. These new ideas, therefore, he assumes to be due to immediate revelation or inspiration from God. Now it is obvious that, even if this inference were well grounded, it assumes that we have somehow arrived independently at a conception of God to which such inspirations can be referred. The Psychology of the human mind cannot assume the existence of such a Being : if we infer such a Being from our own mental experience, that is not immediate but

[1] In *Esquisse d'une Philosophie de la Religion d'après La Psychologie et l'histoire.*

mediate knowledge. It is a belief based on inference,
and a belief which is, properly speaking, metaphysical. The idea of a Religion which is merely
based upon Psychology and involves nothing else
is a delusion : all the great Religions of the world
have been, among other things, metaphysical systems.
We have no means of ascertaining their truth but
Reason, whether it assume the form of a rough
common-sense or of elaborate reasoning which not
only is Metaphysic but knows itself to be so. Reason
is then the organ of religious truth. But then, let
me remind you, Reason includes our moral Reason.
That really is a faculty of immediate knowledge ;
and it is a faculty which, in a higher or lower state
of development, is actually found in practically all
human beings. The one element of truth which I
recognize in the theory of an immediate knowledge
of God is the truth that the most important data
upon which we base the inference which leads to
the knowledge of God are those supplied by the
immediate judgements or intuitions of the Moral
Consciousness.

And here let me caution you against a very preva-
lent misunderstanding about the word Reason. It
is assumed very often that Reason means nothing but
inference. That is not what we mean when we
refer moral judgements to the Reason. We do not
mean that we can prove that things are right or

wrong : we mean precisely the opposite—that
ultimate moral truth is immediate, like the truth
that two and two make four. It might, of course,
be contended that the same Reason which assures
me that goodness is worth having and that the whole
is greater than the part, assures us no less immediately of the existence of God. I can only say that
I am sure I have no such immediate knowledge,
and that for the most part that knowledge is
never claimed by people who understand clearly
the difference between immediate knowledge and
inference. The idea of God is a complex conception,
based, not upon this or that isolated judgement or
momentary experience, but upon the whole of our
experience taken together. It is a hypothesis suggested by, and necessary to, the explanation of our
experience as a whole. Some minds may lay most
stress upon the religious emotions themselves ;
others upon the experience of the outer world, upon
the appearances of design, or upon the metaphysical
argument which shows them the inconceivability
of matter without mind ; others, again, may be most
impressed by the impossibility of accounting in any
way for the immediate consciousness of duty and
the conviction of objective validity or authority
which that consciousness carries with it. But in
any case the knowledge, when it is a reasonable
belief and not based merely upon authority, involves

inference—just like our knowledge of our friend's existence. The fact that my friend is known to me by experience does not prevent his communicating his mind to me. I shall try to show you in my next lecture that to admit that our knowledge of God is based upon inference is not incompatible with the belief that God has spoken to man face to face, as a man speaketh to his friend.

At this point it may perhaps be well, for the sake of clearness, to summarize the position to which I have tried to lead you. I have tried to show that the material Universe cannot reasonably be thought of as having any existence outside, or independently of, Mind. It certainly does not exist merely in any or all of the human and similar minds whose knowledge is fleeting, and which have, there is every reason to believe, a beginning in time. We are bound then to infer the existence of a single Mind or Consciousness, which must be thought of as containing all the elements of our own Consciousness—Reason or Thought, Feeling, and Will— though no doubt in Him those elements or aspects of Consciousness are combined in a manner of which our own minds can give us but a very faint and analogical idea. The world must be thought of as ultimately the thought or experience of this Mind, which we call God. And this Mind must be thought of as not only a Thinker, but also as a Cause or a Will. Our own and all other minds, no less than the events of the material Universe, owe their beginning and continuance to this divine Will : in them the thought or experience of the divine Mind is reproduced in various degrees ; and to all of them is communicated some portion of that causality or activity of which God is the ultimate source, so that their acts must be regarded as due mediately to them, ultimately to God. But, though these minds are wholly dependent upon and in intimate connexion with the divine Mind, they cannot be regarded as *parts* of the divine Consciousness. Reality consists of God and all the minds that He wills to exist, together with the world of Nature which exists in and for those minds. Reality is the system or society of spirits and their experience. The character and ultimate purpose of the divine Mind is revealed to us, however inadequately or imperfectly, in the moral consciousness ; and the moral ideal which is thus communicated to us makes it reasonable for us to expect, for at least the higher of the dependent or created minds, a continuance, of their individual existence, after physical death. Pain, sin, and other evils must be regarded as necessary incidents in the process by which the divine Will is bringing about the greatest attainable good of all conscious beings. The question whether our material Universe, con-

sidered as the object of Mind, has a beginning and
will have an end, is one which we have no data for
deciding. Time-distinctions, I think, must be regarded
as objective—that is to say, as forming part of the
nature and constitution of the real world ; but the
antinomy involved either in supposing an endless
succession or a beginning and end of the time-series
is one which our intellectual faculties are, or at least
have so far proved, incapable of solving. The
element of inadequacy and uncertainty which the
admission of this antinomy introduces into our
theory of the Universe is an emphatic reminder to
us of the inadequate and imperfect character of all
our knowledge. The knowledge, however, that we
possess, though inadequate knowledge, is real knowledge—not a sham knowledge of merely relative or
human validity ; and is sufficient not only for the
guidance of life but even for the partial, though
not the complete, satisfaction of one of the noblest
impulses of the human mind—the disinterested
passion for truth. ' Now we see in a mirror
darkly ' ; but still we see.

The view of the Universe which I have endeavoured
very inadequately to set before you is a form of
Idealism. Inasmuch as it recognizes the existence
—though not the separate and independent existence—of many persons ; inasmuch as it regards
both God and man as persons, without attempting

to merge the existence of either in one all-including, comprehensive consciousness, it may further be described as a form of 'personal Idealism.' But, if any one finds it easier to think of material Nature as having an existence which, though dependent upon and willed by the divine Mind, is not simply an existence in and for mind, such a view of the Universe will serve equally well as a basis of Religion. For religious purposes it makes no difference whether we think of Nature as existing in the Mind of God, or as simply created or brought into and kept in existence by that Mind. When you have subtracted from the theistic case every argument that depends for its force upon the theory that the idea of matter without Mind is an unthinkable absurdity, enough will remain to show the unreasonableness of supposing that in point of fact matter ever has existed without being caused and controlled by Mind. The argument for Idealism may, I hope, have at all events exhibited incidentally the groundlessness and improbability of materialistic and naturalistic assumptions, and left the way clear for the establishment of Theism by the arguments which rest upon the discovery that Causality implies volition; upon the appearances of intelligence in organic life; upon the existence of the moral consciousness; and more generally upon the enormous probability that the ultimate Source of Reality should resemble rather the highest than the lowest kind of existence of which we have experience. That Reality as a whole may be most reasonably interpreted by Reality at its highest is after all the sum and substance of all theistic arguments. If anybody finds it easier to think of matter as uncreated but as always guided and controlled by Mind, I do not think there will be any religious objection to such a position; though it is, as it seems to me, intellectually a less unassailable position than is afforded by an Idealism of the type which I have most inadequately sketched.

Mr. Bradley in a cynical moment has defined Metaphysics as the ' finding of bad reasons for what we believe upon instinct.' I do not for myself accept that definition, which Mr. Bradley himself would not of course regard as expressing the whole truth of the matter. But, though I am firmly convinced that it is possible to find good reasons for the religious beliefs and hopes which have in fact inspired the noblest lives, I still feel that the greatest service which even a little acquaintance with Philosophy may render to many who have not the time for any profounder study of it, will be to give them greater boldness and confidence in accepting a view of the Universe which satisfies the instinctive or unanalysed demands of their moral, intellectual, and spiritual nature.

NOTE ON NON-THEISTIC IDEALISM

It may perhaps be well for the sake of greater clearness to summarize my objections—those already mentioned and some others—to the system of Dr. McTaggart, which I admit to be, for one who has accepted the idealistic position that matter does not exist apart from Mind, the only intelligible alternative to Theism. His theory is, it will be remembered, that ultimate Reality consists of a system of selves or spirits, uncreated and eternal, forming together a Unity, but not a conscious Unity, so that consciousness exists only in the separate selves, not in the whole:

(1) It is admitted that the material world exists only in and for Mind. There is no reason to think that any human mind, or any of the other minds of which Dr. McTaggart's Universe is composed, knows the whole of this world. What kind of existence then have the parts of the Universe which are not known to any mind? It seems to me that Dr. McTaggart would be compelled to admit that they do not exist at all. The world postulated by Science would thus be admitted to be a delusion. This represents a subjective Idealism of an extreme and staggering kind which cannot meet the objections commonly urged against all Idealism.

(2) Moreover, the world is not such an intellectually complete system as Dr. McTaggart insists that it must be, apart from the relations of its known parts to its unknown parts. If there are parts which are unknown to any mind, and which therefore do not exist at all, it is not a system at all.

(3) If it be said that all the spirits between them know the world—one knowing one part, another another—this is a mere hypothesis, opposed to all the probabilities suggested by experience, and after all would be a very inadequate answer to our difficulties. Dr. McTaggart insists

that the world of existing things exists as a system. Such existence to an Idealist must mean existence for a mind ; a system not known as a system to any mind whatever could hardly be said to exist at all.

(4) If it be suggested (as Dr. McTaggart was at one time inclined to suggest) that every mind considered as a timeless Noumenon is omniscient, though in its phenomenal and temporal aspect its knowledge is intermittent and always limited, I reply (a) the theory seems to me not only gratuitous but unintelligible, and (b) it is open to all the difficulties and objections of the theory that time and change are merely subjective delusions. This is too large a question to discuss here : I can only refer to the treatment of the subject by such writers as Lotze (see above) and M. Bergson. I may also refer to Mr. Bradley's argument (*Appearance and Reality*, p. 50 sq.) against the theory that the individual Ego is out of time.

(5) The theory of pre-existent souls is opposed to all the probabilities suggested by experience. Soul and organism are connected in such a way that the pre-existence of one element in what presents itself and works in our world as a unity is an extremely difficult supposition, and involves assumptions which reduce to a minimum the amount of identity or continuity that could be claimed for the Ego throughout its successive lives. A soul which has forgotten all its previous experiences may have some identity with its previous state, but not much. Moreover, we should have to suppose that the correspondence of a certain type of body with a certain kind of soul, as well as the resemblance between the individual and his parents, implies no kind of causal connexion, but is due to mere accident ; or, if it is not to accident, to a very arbitrary kind of pre-established harmony which there is nothing in experience to suggest, and which (upon Dr. McTaggart's theory) there is no creative intelligence to pre-establish. The theory cannot be absolutely refuted, but all Dr. McTaggart's ingenuity has not—to my own mind,

and (I feel sure) to most minds—made it seem otherwise than extremely difficult and improbable. Its sole recommendation is that it makes possible an Idealism without Theism : but, if Theism be an easier and more defensible theory, that is no recommendation at all.

(6) Dr. McTaggart's whole theory seems to me to waver between two inconsistent views of Reality. When he insists that the world consists of a system or Unity, he tends towards a view of things which makes the system of intellectual relations constituting knowledge or Science to be the very reality of things : on such a view there is no impossibility of an ultimate Reality not known to any one mind. But Dr. McTaggart has too strong a hold on the conviction of the supremely real character of conscious mind and the unreality of mere abstractions to be satisfied with this view. If there is no mind which both knows and wills the existence and the mutual relations of the spirits, the supreme reality must be found in the individual spirits themselves ; yet the system, if known to none of them, seems to fall outside the reality. The natural tendency of a system which finds the sole reality in eternally self-existent souls is towards Pluralism—a theory of wholly independent 'Reals' or 'Monads.' Dr. McTaggart is too much of a Hegelian to acquiesce in such a view. The gulf between the two tendencies seems to me—with all respect—to be awkwardly bridged over by the assumption that the separate selves form an intelligible system, which nevertheless no one really existent spirit actually understands. If a system of relations can be Reality, there is no ground for assuming the pre-existence or eternity of individual souls : if on the other hand Reality is 'experience,' an unexperienced 'system' cannot be real, and the 'unity' disappears. This is a line of objection which it would require a much more thorough discussion to develope.

(7) On the view which I myself hold as to the nature of Causality, the only intelligible cause of events is a Will. The events of Dr. McTaggart's world (putting aside the very

small proportion which are due, in part at least, to the voluntary action of men or spirits) are not caused at all. His theory is therefore open to all—and more than all—the objections which I have urged in Lecture II. against the theory which explains the Universe as the thought of a Mind but not as caused by that Mind.

(8) It is just possible that some one might suggest that the first of my objections might be met by the allegation that there is nothing in the scheme which forbids us to suppose that the whole of Nature is known to more than one of the spirits which make up Reality, though not to all, or indeed any, of the human and non-human spirits known to us. I should reply (a) that the considerations which lead to the hypothesis of one omniscient Being do not require more than one such spirit, and *entia non sunt multiplicanda præter necessitatem* ; (b) such a scheme would still be open to Objection 7. If it is a speculative possibility that all Nature may exist in the knowledge of more than one spirit, it cannot well be thought of as willed by more than one spirit. If the Universe, admitted to form an ordered system, is caused by rational will at all, it must surely be caused by one Will. But perhaps a serious discussion of a polytheistic scheme such as this may be postponed till it is seriously maintained. It has not been suggested, so far as I am aware, by Dr. McTaggart himself.

(9) The real strength of Dr. McTaggart's system must be measured by the validity of his objections to a Theism such as I have defended. I have attempted to reply to those objections in the course of these Lectures, and more at length in a review of his *Some Dogmas of Religion* in *Mind* (N.S.), vol. xv., 1906.

LECTURE V

REVELATION

I HAVE tried in previous lectures to show that the apprehension of religious truth does not depend upon some special kind of intuition; that it is not due to some special faculty superior to and different in kind from our ordinary intellectual activities, but to an exercise of the same intellectual faculties by which we attain to truth in other matters—including, however, especially the wholly unique faculty of immediately discerning values or pronouncing moral judgements. The word 'faith' should, as it seems to me, be used to express not a mysterious capacity for attaining to knowledge without thought or without evidence, but to indicate some of the manifold characteristics by which our religious knowledge is distinguished from the knowledge either of common life or of the physical Sciences. If I had time there would be much to be said about these characteristics, and I think I could show that the popular distinction between knowledge and religious

faith finds whatever real justification it possesses
in these characteristics of religious knowledge. I
might insist on the frequently implicit and unanalysed
character of religious thinking ; upon the incom-
pleteness and inadequacy of even the fullest account
that the maturest and acutest Philosopher can give
of ultimate Reality ; upon the merely probable and
analogical character of much of the reasoning which
is necessarily employed both in the most popular
and in the most philosophical kinds of reasoning
about such matters; and above all upon the prominent
place which moral judgements occupy in religious
thought, moral judgements which, on account of their
immediate character and their emotional setting, are
often not recognized in their true character as judgements of the Reason. Most of the mistakes into which
popular thinking has fallen in this matter—the
mistakes which culminate in the famous examina-
tion-paper definition of faith as ' a means of believing
that which we know not to be true '—would be
avoided if we would only remember, with St. Paul
and most of the greater religious thinkers, that the
true antithesis is not between faith and reason but
between faith and sight. All religious belief implies
a belief in something which cannot be touched or
tasted or handled, and which cannot be established
by any mere logical deduction from what can be
touched or tasted or handled. So far from implying

scepticism as to the power of Reason, this opposition
between faith and sight actually asserts the possibility of attaining by thought to a knowledge of
realities which cannot be touched or tasted or
handled—a knowledge of equal validity and trust-
worthiness with that which is popularly said to be
due to the senses, though Plato has taught us once
for all[1] that the senses by themselves never give us
real knowledge, and that in the apprehension of the
most ordinary matter of fact there is implied the
action of the self-same intellect by which alone we
can reach the knowledge of God.

It may further be pointed out that, though neither
religious knowledge nor moral knowledge are mere
emotion, they are both of them very closely connected
with certain emotions. Great moral discoveries are
made, not so much by superior intellectual power,
as by superior interest in the subject-matter of
Morality. Very ordinary intelligence can see, when
it is really brought to bear upon the matter, the
irrationality or immorality of bad customs, oppres-
sions, social injustices ; but the people who have
led the revolt against these things have generally
been the people who have felt intensely about them.
So it is with the more distinctly religious knowledge. Religious thought and insight are largely
dependent upon the emotions to which religious

[1] Throughout his writings, but pre-eminently in the *Theœtetus*.

ideas and beliefs appeal. The absence of religious
thought and definite religious belief is very often
(I am far from saying always) due to a want of
interest in Religion ; but that does not prove that
religious thought is not the work of the intellect,
any more than the fact that a man is ignorant of
Politics because he takes no interest in Politics
proves that political truth is a mere matter of
emotion, and has nothing to do with the understanding. Thought is always guided by interest—
a truth which must not be distorted with a certain
modern school of thought, if indeed it can properly
be called thought, into the assertion that thinking
is nothing but willing, and that therefore we are at
liberty to think just what we please.

And that leads on to a further point. Emotion
and desire are very closely connected with the will.
A man's moral insight and the development of his
thought about moral questions depend very largely
upon the extent to which he acts up to whatever light
he has. Vice, as Aristotle put it, is φθαρτικὴ ἀρχῆς
—destructive of moral first principles. Moral insight
is largely dependent upon character. And so is
religious insight. Thus it is quite true to say that
religious belief depends in part upon the state of
the will. This doctrine has been so scandalously
abused by many Theologians and Apologists that
I use it with great hesitation. I have no sympathy

with the idea that we are justified in believing a religious doctrine merely because we wish it to be true, or with the insinuation that non-belief in a religious truth is always or necessarily due to moral obliquity. But still it is undeniable that a man's ethical and religious beliefs are to some extent affected by the state of his will. That is so with all knowledge to some extent; for progress in knowledge requires attention, and is largely dependent upon interest. If I take no interest in the properties of curves or the square root of −1, I am not very likely to make a good mathematician. This connexion of knowledge with interest applies in an exceptional degree to religious knowledge : and that is one of the points which I think many religious thinkers have intended to emphasize by their too hard and fast distinctions between faith and knowledge.

Belief itself is thus to some extent affected by the state of the will; and still more emphatically does the extent to which belief affects action depend upon the will. Many beliefs which we quite sincerely hold are what have been called ' otiose beliefs '; we do not by an effort of the will realize them sufficiently strongly for them to affect action. Many a man knows perfectly that his course of life will injure or destroy his physical health; it is not through intellectual scepticism that he disobeys his physician's prescriptions, but because other desires and inclinations prevent his attending to them and acting upon them. It is obvious that to men like St. Paul and Luther faith meant much more than a mere state of the intellect; it included a certain emotional and a certain volitional attitude; it included love and it included obedience. Whether our intellectual beliefs about Religion are energetic enough to influence action, does to an enormous extent depend upon our wills. Faith is, then, used, and almost inevitably used, in such a great variety of senses that I do not like to lay down one definite and exclusive definition of it; but it would be safe to say that, for many purposes and in many connexions, religious faith means the deliberate adoption by an effort of the will, as practically certain for purposes of action and of feeling, of a religious belief which to the intellect is, or may be, merely probable. For purposes of life it is entirely reasonable to treat probabilities as certainties. If a man has reason to think his friend is trustworthy, he will do well to trust him wholly and implicitly. If a man has reason to think that a certain view of the Universe is the most probable one, he will do well habitually to allow that conviction to dominate not merely his actions, but the habitual tenour of his emotional and spiritual life. We should not love a human being much if we allowed ourselves habitually to contemplate the logical possibility that the loved one was unworthy of, or irresponsive to, our affection. We could not love God if we habitually contemplated the fact that His existence rests for us upon judgements in which there is more or less possibility of error, though there is no reason why we should, in our speculative moments, claim a greater certainty for them than seems to be reasonable. The doctrine that 'probability is the guide of life' is one on which every sensible man habitually acts in all other relations of life: Bishop Butler was right in contending that it should be applied no less unhesitatingly to the matter of religious belief and religious aspiration.

The view which I have taken of the nature of faith may be illustrated by the position of Clement of Alexandria. It is clear from his writings that by faith he meant a kind of conviction falling short of demonstration or immediate intellectual insight, and dependent in part upon the state of the will and the heart. Clement did not disparage knowledge in the interests of faith: faith was to him a more elementary kind of knowledge resting largely upon moral conviction, and the foundation of that higher state of intellectual apprehension which he called Gnosis. I do not mean, of course, to adopt Clement's Philosophy as a whole ; I merely refer to it as illustrating the point that, properly considered, faith is, or rather includes, a particular kind or stage of knowledge, and is not a totally different and even opposite state of mind. It would be easy to show that this has been fully recognized by many, if not most, of the great Christian thinkers.

One last point. It is of the utmost importance to distinguish between the process by which psychologically a man arrives at a religious or other truth and the reasons which make it true. Because I deny that the truth of God's existence can reasonably be accepted on the basis of an immediate judgement or intuition, I do not deny for one moment that an apparently intuitive conviction of the truth of Christianity, as of other religions, actually exists. The religious belief of the vast majority of persons has always rested, and must always rest, very largely upon tradition, education, environment, authority of one kind or another—authority supported or confirmed by a varying measure of independent reflection or experience. And, just where the influence of authority is most complete and overwhelming, it is least felt to be authority. The person whose beliefs are most entirely produced by education or environment is very often most convinced that his opinions are due solely to his own immediate insight. But even where this is not the case—even where the religious man is taking a new departure, revolting against his environment and adopting a religious belief absolutely at variance with the established

belief of his society—I do not contend that such new
religious ideas are always due to unobserved and
unanalysed processes of reasoning. That in most
cases, when a person adopts a new creed, he would
himself give some reason for his change of faith is
obvious, though the reason which he would allege
would not in all cases be the one which really caused
the change of religion. There may be other
psychological influences which cause belief besides
the influence of environment : in some cases the
psychological causes of such beliefs are altogether
beyond analysis. But, though I do not think
M. Auguste Sabatier justified in assuming that a
belief is true, and must come directly from God,
simply because we cannot easily explain its genesis
by the individual's environment and psychological
antecedents, it is of extreme importance to insist
that it is not proved to be false because it was not
adopted primarily, or at all, on adequate theoretical
grounds. A belief which arose at first entirely
without logical justification, or it may be on intellectual grounds subsequently discovered to be
inadequate or false, may nevertheless be one which
can and does justify itself to the reflective intellect
of the person himself or of other persons. And
many new, true, and valuable beliefs have undoubtedly arisen in this way. Even in physical Science
we all know that there is no Logic of discovery. It

is a familiar criticism upon the Logic of Bacon that
he ignored or under-estimated the part that is played
in scientific thinking by hypothesis, and the consequent need of scientific imagination. Very often the
new scientific idea comes into the discoverer's mind,
he knows not how or why. Some great man of Science
—I think, Helmholtz—said of a brilliant discovery
of his, 'It was given to me.' But it was not true
because it came to Helmholtz in this way, but
because it was subsequently verified and proved.
Now, undoubtedly, religious beliefs, new and old,
often do present themselves to the minds of individuals in an intuitive and unaccountable way. They
may subsequently be justified at the bar of Reason :
and yet Reason might never have discovered them
for itself. They would never have come into the
world unless they had presented themselves at first
to some mind or other as intuitions, inspirations,
immediate Revelations : and yet (once again) the
fact that they so present themselves does not by itself
prove them to be true.

I may perhaps illustrate what I mean by the
analogy of Poetry. I suppose few people will push
the sound-without-sense view of Poetry to the
length of denying that poets do sometimes see and
teach us truths. No one—least of all one who is
not even a verse-maker himself—can, I suppose,
analyse the intellectual process by which a poet

gets at his truths. The insight by which he arrives at them is closely connected with emotions of various kinds : and yet the truths are not themselves emotions, nor do they in all cases merely state the fact that the poet has felt such and such emotions. They are propositions about the nature of things, not merely about the poet's mental states. And yet the truths are not true because the poet *feels* them, as he would say—no matter how passionately he feels them. There is no separate organ of poetic truth : and not all the things that poets have passionately felt are true. Some highly poetical thoughts have been very false thoughts. But, if they are true, they must be true for good logical reasons, which a philosophical critic may even in some cases by subsequent reflection be able to disentangle and set forth. Yet the poet did not get at those truths by way of philosophical reflection : or, if he was led to them by any logical process, he could not have analysed his own reasoning. The poet could not have produced the arguments of the philosopher : the philosopher without the poet's lead might never have seen the truth. I am afraid I must not stay to defend or illustrate this position : I will only say that the poets I should most naturally go to for illustration would be such poets as Wordsworth, Tennyson, and Browning, though perhaps all three are a little too consciously philosophic to supply the ideal illustration.

I do not think it will be difficult to apply these reflections to the case of religious and ethical truth. All religious truth, as I hold, depends logically upon inference; inference from the whole body of our experiences, among which the most important place is held by our immediate moral judgements. The truth of Theism is in that sense a truth discernible by Reason. But it does not follow that, when it was first discovered, it was arrived at by the inferences which I have endeavoured to some extent to analyse, or by one of the many lines of thought which may lead to the same conclusions. It was not the Greek philosophers so much as the Jewish prophets who taught the world true Monotheism. Hosea, Amos, the two Isaiahs probably arrived at their Monotheism largely by intuition; or (in so far as it was by inferential processes) the premisses of their argument were very probably inherited beliefs of earlier Judaism which would not commend themselves without qualification to a modern thinker. In its essentials the Monotheism of Isaiah is a reasonable belief; we accept it because it is reasonable, not because Isaiah had an intuition that it was true; for we have rejected many things which to Isaiah probably seemed no less self-evidently true. And yet it would be a profound mistake to assume that

the philosophers who now defend Isaiah's creed
would ever have arrived at it without Isaiah's aid.

I hope that by this time you will have seen to
some extent the spirit in which I am approaching
the special subject of to-day's lecture—the question
of Revelation. In some of the senses that have
been given to it, the idea of Revelation is one which
hardly any one trained in the school—that is to say,
any school—of modern Philosophy is likely to
accept. The idea that pieces of information have
been supernaturally and without any employment
of their own intellectual faculties communicated at
various times to particular persons, their truth being
guaranteed by miracles—in the sense of interruptions
of the ordinary course of nature by an extraordinary
fiat of creative power—is one which is already
rejected by most modern theologians, even among
those who would generally be called rather conserva-
tive theologians. I will not now argue the question
whether any miraculous event, however well attested,
could possibly be sufficient evidence for the truth
of spiritual teaching given in attestation of it. I
will merely remark that to any one who has really
appreciated the meaning of biblical criticism, it is
scarcely conceivable that the evidence for miracles
could seem sufficiently cogent to constitute such an
attestation. In proof of that I will merely appeal
to the modest, apologetic, tentative tone in which

scholarly and sober-minded theologians who would
usually be classed among the defenders of miracles—
men like the Bishop of Ely or Professor Sanday of
Oxford—are content to speak of such evidences.
They admit the difficulty of proving that such
miraculous events really happened thousands of
years ago on the strength of narratives written at
the very earliest fifty years after the alleged event,
and they invite us rather to believe in the miracles
on the evidence of a Revelation already accepted
than to accept the revelation on the evidence of the
miracles.   I shall have a word to say on this question
of miracles next time ; but for the present I want
to establish, or rather without much argument to
put before you for your consideration, this position ;
that the idea of revelation cannot be admitted in
the sense of a communication of truth by God, claiming to be accepted not on account of its own intrinsic
reasonableness or of the intellectual or spiritual
insight of the person to whom it is made, but on
account of the historical evidence for miraculous
occurrences said to have taken place in connexion
with such communication. The most that can
reasonably be contended for, is that super-normal
occurrences of this kind may possess a certain
corroborative value in support of a Revelation
claiming to be accepted on other grounds.

What place then is left for the idea of Revelation ?

I will ask you to go back for a moment to the conclusions of our first lecture. We saw that from the
idealistic point of view all knowledge may be looked
upon as a partial communication to the human
soul of the thoughts or experiences of the divine
Mind. There is a sense then in which all truth is
revealed truth. In a more important sense, and a
sense more nearly allied to that of ordinary usage,
all moral and spiritual truth may be regarded as
revealed truth. And in particular those immediate
judgements about good and evil in which we have
found the sole means of knowing the divine character
and purposes must be looked on as divinely implanted knowledge—none the less divinely implanted
because it is, in the ordinary sense of the words,
quite natural, normal, and consistent with law.
Nobody but an Atheist ought to talk about the un-
assisted human intellect : no one who acquiesces
in the old doctrine that Conscience is the voice of
God ought either on the one hand to deny the
existence of Revelation, or on the other to speak of
Revelation as if it were confined to the Bible.

But because we ascribe some intrinsic power of
judging about spiritual and moral matters to the
ordinary human intellect, it would be a grievous
mistake to assume that all men have an equal
measure of this power. Because we assert that all
moral and spiritual truth comes to men by Revela-

tion, it does not follow that there are not degrees of Revelation. And it is one of the special characteristics of religious and moral truth that it is in a peculiar degree dependent upon the superior insight of those exceptional men to whom have been accorded extraordinary degrees of moral and spiritual insight. Even in Science, as we have seen, we cannot dispense with genius : very ordinary men can satisfy themselves of the truth of a hypothesis when it is once suggested, though they would have been quite incompetent to discover that hypothesis for themselves. Still more unquestionably are there moral and spiritual truths which, when once discovered, can be seen to be true by men of very commonplace intellect and commonplace character. The truths are seen and passed on to others, who accept them partly on authority, by way of social inheritance and tradition; partly because they are confirmed in various degrees by their own independent judgement and experience. Here then—in the discovery of new spiritual truth—we encounter that higher and exceptional degree of spiritual and ethical insight which in a special and pre-eminent sense we ought to regard as Revelation or Inspiration. Here there is room, in the evolution of Religion and Morality, for the influence of the men of moral or religious genius—the Prophets, the Apostles, the Founders and Reformers of Religions : and, since

moral and spiritual insight are very closely connected
with character, for the moral hero, the leader of men,
the Saint. Especially to the new departures, the
turning-points, the epoch-making discoveries in
ethical and religious progress connected with the
appearance of such men, we may apply the term
Revelation in a supreme or culminating sense.

It is, as it seems to me, extremely important that
we should not altogether divorce the idea of Revelation from those kinds of moral and religious truth
which are arrived at by the ordinary working of the
human intellect. The ultimate moral judgements
no doubt must be intuitive or immediate, but in our
deductions from them—in their application both
to practical life and to theories about God and the
Universe—there is room for much intellectual work
of the kind which we commonly associate rather
with the philosopher than with the prophet. But
the philosopher may be also a prophet. The philosophically trained Greek Fathers were surely right
in recognizing that men like Socrates and Plato
were to be numbered among those to whom the
Spirit of God had spoken in an exceptional degree.
They too spoke in the power of the indwelling Logos.
But still it is quite natural that we should associate
the idea of Revelation or Inspiration more particularly with that kind of moral and intellectual
discovery which comes to exceptional men by way

of apparent intuition or immediate insight. We
associate the idea of inspiration rather with the poet
than with the man of Science, and with the prophet
rather than with the systematic philosopher. It
is quite natural, therefore, that we should associate
the idea of Revelation more especially with religious
teachers of the intuitive order like the Jewish
prophets than with even those philosophers who
have also been great practical teachers of Ethics
and Religion. But it is most important to recognize
that there is no hard and fast line to be drawn
between the two classes. The Jewish prophets did
not arrive at their ideas about God without a great
deal of hard thinking, though the thinking is for
the most part unexplicit and the mode of expression
poetic. 'Their idols are silver and gold; even the
work of men's hands. . . . They have hands and
handle not; feet have they and walk not: neither
speak they through their throat.' There is real hard
reasoning underlying such noble rhetoric, though the
Psalmist could not perhaps have reduced his argument against Polytheism and Idolatry to the form
of a dialectical argument like Plato or St. Thomas
Aquinas. In the highest instance of all—the case
of our Lord Jesus Christ himself—a natural instinct
of reverence is apt to deter us from analysing how
he came by the truth that he communicated to men;
but, though I would not deny that the deepest

truth came to him chiefly by a supreme gift of intuition, there are obvious indications of profound intellectual thought in his teaching. Recall for a moment his arguments against the misuse of the Sabbath, against the superstition of unclean meats, against the Sadducean objection to the Resurrection. I want to avoid at present dogmatic phraseology; so I will only submit in passing that this is only what we should expect if the early Church was right in thinking of Christ as the supreme expression in the moral and religious sphere of the Logos or Reason of God.

The thought of great religious thinkers is none the less Revelation because it involves the use of their reasoning faculties. But I guarded myself against being supposed, in contending for the possibility of a philosophical or metaphysical knowledge of God, to assume that religious truth had always come to men in this way, or even that the greatest steps in religious progress have usually taken the form of explicit reasoning. Once again, it is all-important to distinguish between the way in which a belief comes to be entertained and the reasons for its being true. All sorts of psychological causes have contributed to generate religious beliefs. And when once we have discovered grounds in our own reflection or experience for believing them to be true, there is no reason why we should not regard all of them as pieces of divine revelation. Visions and dreams, for instance, had a share in the development of religious ideas. We might even admit the possibility that the human race would never have been led to think of the immortality of the soul but for primitive ideas about ghosts suggested by the phenomena of dreams. The truth of the doctrine is neither proved nor disproved by such an account of its origin ; but, if that belief is true and dreams have played a part in the process by which man has been led to it, no Theist surely can refuse to recognize the divine guidance therein. And so, at a higher level, we are told by the author of the Acts that St. Peter was led to accept the great principle of Gentile Christianity by the vision of a sheet let down from heaven. There is no reason why that account should not be historically true. The psychologist may very easily account for St. Peter's vision by the working in his mind of the liberal teaching of Stephen, the effect of his fast, and so on. But that does not prevent us recognizing that vision as an instrument of divine Revelation. We at the present day do not believe in this fundamental principle of Christianity because of that dream of St. Peter's ; for we know that dreams are not always truth or always edifying. We believe in that principle on other grounds—the convincing grounds (among others) which St. Luke puts into St. Peter's mouth

on the following morning. But that need not prevent our recognizing that God may have communicated that truth to the men of that generation—and
through them to us—partly by means of that dream.

The two principles then for which I wish to
contend are these : (1) that Revelation is a matter of
degree ; (2) that no Revelation can be accepted in
the long run merely because it came to a particular
person in a peculiarly intuitive or immediate way.
It may be that M. Auguste Sabatier is right in seeing
the most immediate contact of God with the human
soul in those intuitive convictions which can least
easily be accounted for by ordinary psychological
causes; in those new departures of religious insight,
those unaccountable comings of new thoughts into
the mind, which constitute the great crises or turning-
points of religious history.   But, though the coming
of such thoughts may often be accepted by the
individual as direct evidences of a divine origin, the
Metaphysician, on looking back upon them, cannot
treat the fact that the psychologist cannot account
for them, as a convincing proof of such an origin,
apart from our judgement upon the contents of what
claims to be a revelation.   Untrue thoughts and
wicked thoughts sometimes arise equally unaccountably : the fact that they do so is even now
accounted for by some as a sufficient proof of direct
diabolic suggestion.   When we have judged the

thought to be true or the suggestion to be good, then we, who on other grounds believe in God, may see in it a piece of divine revelation, but not till then.

From this point of view it is clear that we are able to recognize various degrees and various kinds of divine revelation in many different Religions, philosophies, systems of ethical teaching. We are able to recognize the importance to the world of the great historical Religions, in all of which we can acknowledge a measure of Revelation. The fact that the truths which they teach (in so far as they are true) can now be recognized as true by philosophic thought, does not show that the world would ever have evolved those thoughts, apart from the influence of the great revealing personalities. Philosophy itself—the Philosophy of the professed philosophers—has no doubt contributed a very important element to the content of the historical Religions; but it is only in proportion as they become part of a system of religious teaching, and the possession of an organized religious community, that the ideas of the philosophers really come home to multitudes of men, and shape the history of the world. Nor in many cases would the philosophers themselves have seen what they have seen but for the great epoch-making thoughts of the great religion-making periods. And the same considerations which show the importance of religious movements in the past tend also to emphasize the importance of the historical Religion and of the religious community in which it is enshrined in modern times. Because religious truth can now be defended by the use of our ordinary intellectual faculties, and because all possess these faculties in some degree, it is absurd to suppose that the ordinary individual, if left to himself, would be likely to evolve a true religious system for himself—any more than he would be likely to discern for himself the truths that were first seen by Euclid or Newton if he were not taught them. To under-estimate the importance of the great historical Religions and their creators has been the besetting sin of technical religious Philosophy. Metaphysicians have in truth often written about Religion in great ignorance as to the real facts of religious history.

But because we recognize a measure of truth in all the historical Religions, it does not follow that we can recognize an equal amount of truth in all of them. The idea that all the Religions teach much the same thing—or that, while they vary about that unimportant part of Religion which is called doctrine or dogma, they are all agreed about Morality—is an idea which could only occur to the self-complaisant ignorance which of late years has done most of the theological writing in the correspondence columns of our newspapers. The real student of comparative

Religion knows that it is only at a rather advanced stage in the development of Religion that
Religion becomes in any important degree an ethical
teacher at all. Even the highest and most ethical
Religions are not agreed either in their Ethics or in
their Theology. Not only can we recognize higher
and lower Religions; but the highest Religions,
among many things which they have in common,
are at certain points diametrically antagonistic to
each other. It is impossible therefore reasonably
to maintain that fashionable attitude of mind
towards these Religions which my friend Professor
Inge once described as a sort of honorary member-
ship of all Religions except one's own. If we are
to regard the historical Religions as being of any
importance to our own personal religious life, we
must choose between them. If we put aside the
case of Judaism in its most cultivated modern form,
a form in which it has been largely influenced by
Christianity, I suppose there is practically only one
Religion which would be in the least likely to appeal
to a modern philosophical student of Religion as
a possible alternative to Christianity—and that is
Buddhism. But Buddhist Ethics are not the same
as Christian Ethics. Buddhist Ethics are ascetic :
the Christianity which Christ taught was anti-
ascetic. In its view of the future, Buddhism is
pessimistic ; Christianity is optimistic. Much as

Buddhism has done to inculcate Humanity and Charity, the principle of Buddhist Humanity is not the same as that of Christianity. Humanity is encouraged by the Buddhist (in so far as he is really influenced by his own formal creed) not from a motive of disinterested affection, but as a means of escaping from the evils of personal and individual existence, and so winning Nirvana. We cannot at one and the same time adhere to the Ethics of Buddhism and to those of Christianity, though I am far from saying that Christians have nothing to learn either from Buddhist teaching or from Buddhist practice. Still less can we at one and the same time be Atheists with the Buddhist and Theists with the Christian ; look forward with the Buddhist to the extinction of personal consciousness and with the Christian to a fuller and more satisfying life. To take an interest in comparative Religion is not to be religious ; to be religious implies a certain exclusive attachment to some definite form of religious belief, though it may of course often be a belief to which many historical influences have contributed.

I have been trying to lead you to a view of Revelation which recognizes the existence and the importance of those exceptional religious minds to whom is due the foundation and development of the great historical Religions, while at the same time we refuse, in the last resort, to recognize any revela-

tion as true except on the ground that its truth can
be independently verified. I do not mean to deny
that the individual must at first, and may quite
reasonably in some cases throughout life, accept
much of his religious belief on authority; but that
is only because he may be justified in thinking that
such and such a person, or more probably such and
such a religious community, is more likely to be
right than himself. Rational submission to authority
in this or that individual postulates independent
judgement on the part of others. I am far
from saying that every individual is bound to
satisfy himself by personal enquiry as to the truth
of every element in his own Religion; but, if and
so far as he determines to do so, he cannot reasonably
accept an alleged revelation on any other ground
than that it comes home to him, that the content
of that Religion appeals to him as true, as satisfying
the demands of his intellect and of his conscience.
The question in which most of us, I imagine, are
most vitally interested is whether the Christian
Religion is a Religion which we can accept on these
grounds. That it possesses some truth, that whatever in it is true comes from God—that much is
likely to be admitted by all who believe in any
kind of Religion in the sense in which we have been
discussing Religion. The great question for us is,
' Can we find any reason for the modern man identi-

fying himself in any exclusive way with the historical
Christian Religion ?   Granted that there is some
truth in all Religions, does Christianity contain the
most truth ?   Is it in any sense the one absolute,
final, universal Religion ? '

That will be the subject for our consideration in
the next lecture.   But meanwhile I want to suggest
to you one very broad provisional answer to our
problem.   Christianity alone of the historical Religions teaches those great truths to which we have
been conducted by a mere appeal to Reason and to
Conscience.   It teaches ethical Monotheism ; that is
to say, it thinks of God as a thinking, feeling, willing
Consciousness, and understands His nature in the
light of the highest moral ideal.   It teaches the belief
in personal Immortality, and it teaches a Morality
which in its broad general principles still appeals to
the Conscience of Humanity.   Universal Love it sets
forth as at once the central point in its moral ideal
and the most important element in its conception
of God.   In one of those metaphors which express
so much more than any more exact philosophical
formula, it is the Religion which teaches the Fatherhood of God and the brotherhood of man.   And
these truths were taught by the historical Jesus.
No one up to his time had ever taught them with
equal clearness and in equal purity, and with the
same freedom from other and inconsistent teachings :

and this teaching was developed by his first followers. Amid all aberrations and amid all contamination by heterogeneous elements, the society or societies which look back to Christ as their Founder have never in the worst times ceased altogether to teach these truths ; and now they more and more tend to constitute the essence of Christianity as it is to-day —all the more so on account of the Church's gradual shuffling off of so many adventitious ideas and practices which were at one time associated with them. Christianity is and remains the only one of the great historical Religions which has taught and does teach these great truths in all their fullness.[1] These considerations would by themselves be sufficient to put Christianity in an absolutely unique position among the Religions of Mankind.

I have so far been regarding our Lord Jesus Christ simply as a teacher of religious and ethical truth. I think it is of fundamental importance that we should *begin* by regarding him in this light.

---

[1] If it be said that Judaism or any other Religion does now teach these truths as fully as Christianity, this may possibly apply to the creed of individual members of these Religions, but it can hardly be claimed for the historical Religions themselves. I should certainly be prepared to contend that even such individuals lose something by not placing in the centre of their Religion the personality of him by whom they were first taught, and the communities which have been the great transmitters of them. But in this course of lectures I am chiefly concerned with giving reasons why Christians should remain Christians, rather than with giving reasons why others who are not so should become Christians.

It was in this light that he first presented himself
to his fellow-countrymen—even before (in all
probability) he claimed to be the fulfiller of the
Messianic ideal which had been set before them by
the prophets of their race. And I could not, without
a vast array of quotation, give you a sufficient
impression of the prominence of this aspect of his
work and personality among the earlier Greek
Fathers. Even after the elaborate doctrines of
Catholic Christianity had begun to be developed,
it was still primarily as the supremely inspired
Teacher that Jesus was most often thought of.
When the early Christians thought of him as the
incarnate Logos or Reason of God, to teach men
divine truth was still looked upon as the supreme
function of the Logos and the purpose of his in-
dwelling in the historical Jesus. But from the
first Jesus appealed to men as much more than a
teacher. It is one of the distinctive peculiarities
of religious and ethical knowledge that it is inti-
mately connected with character : religious and
moral teaching of the highest kind is in a peculiar
degree inseparable from the personality of the
teacher. Jesus impressed his contemporaries, and
he has impressed successive ages as having not only
set before man the highest religious and moral
ideal, but as having in a unique manner realized
that ideal in his own life. Even the word ' example '

does not fully express the impression which he made on his followers, or do justice to the inseparability of his personality from his teaching. In the religious consciousness of Christ men saw realized the ideal relation of man not merely to his fellow-man but also to his heavenly Father. From the first an enthusiastic reverence for its Founder has been an essential part of the Christian Religion amid all the variety of the phases which it has assumed. The doctrine of the Christian Church was in its origin an attempt to express in the philosophical language of the time its sense of this supreme value of Christ for the religious and moral life of man. As to the historical success and the present usefulness of these attempts, I shall have a word to say next time. Meanwhile, I would leave with you this one thought. The claim of Christianity to be the supreme, the universal, in a sense the final Religion, must rest mainly, in the last resort, upon the appeal which Christ and his Religion make to the moral and religious consciousness of the present.

LITERATURE

See the works mentioned at the end of the next Lecture, to which, as dealing more specially with the subject of Lecture v., may be added Professor Sanday's *Inspiration*, and Professor Wendt's *Revelation and Christianity*.

LECTURE VI

CHRISTIANITY

IN my last lecture I tried to effect a transition from the idea of religious truth as something believed by the individual, and accepted by him on the evidence of his own Reason and Conscience to the idea of *a* Religion considered as a body of religious truth handed down by tradition in an organized society. The higher Religions—those which have passed beyond the stage of merely tribal or national Religion —are based upon the idea that religious truth of enduring value has been from time to time revealed to particular persons, the Founders or Apostles or Reformers of such religions. We recognized the validity of this idea of Revelation, and the supreme importance to the moral and religious life of such historical revelations, on one condition—that the claim of any historical Religion to the allegiance of its followers must be held to rest in the last resort upon the appeal which it makes to their Reason and Conscience : though the individual may often be

quite Justified in accepting and relying upon the
Reason and Conscience of the religious Society rather
than upon his own.

The view which I have taken of Revelation makes
it quite independent of what are commonly called
miracles. All that I have said is quite consistent
with the unqualified acceptance or with the unqualified rejection of miracles. But some of you
may perhaps expect me to explain a little more fully
my own attitude towards that question. And therefore I will say this much—that, if we regard a
miracle as implying a suspension of a law of nature,
I do not think we can call such a suspension
a priori incredible ; but the enormous experience
which we have of the actual regularity of the laws
of nature, and of the causes which in certain states
of the human mind lead to the belief in miracles,
makes such an event in the highest degree improbable. To me at least it would seem practically
impossible to get sufficient evidence for the occurrence
of such an event in the distant past : all our historical
reasoning presupposes the reign of law. But it is
being more and more admitted by theologians who
are regarded as quite orthodox and rather con-
servative, that the idea of a miracle need not necessarily imply such a suspension of natural law. And
on the other hand, decidedly critical and liberal
theologians are more and more disposed to admit

that many of the abnormal events commonly called miraculous may very well have occurred without involving any real suspension of natural law. Recent advances in psychological knowledge have widened our conception of the possible influence of mind over matter and of mind over mind. Whether an alleged miraculous event is to be accepted or not must, as it seems to me, depend partly upon the amount of critically sifted historical evidence which can be produced for it, partly upon the nature of the event itself—upon the question whether it is or is not of such a kind that we can with any probability suppose that it might be accounted for either by known laws or by laws at present imperfectly understood.

To apply these principles in detail to the New Testament narratives would involve critical discussions which are outside the purpose of these lectures. I will only say that few critical scholars would deny that some recorded miracles even in the New Testament are unhistorical. When they find an incident like the healing of Malchus's ear omitted in the earlier, and inserted in the later redaction of a common original, they cannot but recognize the probability of traditional amplification. At the same time few liberal theologians will be disposed to doubt the general fact that our Lord did cure some diseases by spiritual influence, or that an appearance of our Lord to the disciples—of whatever nature—actually

did occur, and was the means of assuring them of
his continued life and power. At all events I do
not myself doubt these two facts. But at least
when miracles are not regarded as constituting real
exceptions to natural law, it is obvious that they
will not prove the truth of any teaching which may
have been connected with them; while, even if we
treat the Gospel miracles as real exceptions to law,
the difficulty of proving them in the face of modern
critical enquiry is so great that the evidence will
hardly come home to any one not previously convinced, on purely spiritual grounds, of the exceptional character of our Lord's personality and
mission. This being so, I do not think that our
answer to the problem of miracles, whatever it be,
can play any very important part in Christian
Apologetic. When we have become Christians on
other grounds, the acts of healing may still retain
a certain value as illustrating the character of the
Master, and the Resurrection vision as proclaiming
the truth of Immortality in a way which will
come home to minds not easily accessible to
abstract argument. The true foundation not merely
for belief in the teaching of Christ, but also for
the Christian's reverence for his Person, must, as
it seems to me, be found in the appeal which his
words and his character still make to the Conscience
and Reason of mankind. This proposition would be

perhaps more generally accepted if I were to say
that the claim of Christ to allegiance rests upon the
way in which he satisfies the heart, the aspirations,
the religious needs of mankind. And I should be
quite willing to adopt such language, if you will
only include respect for historic fact and intellectual
truth among these religious needs, and admit that
a reasonable faith must rest on something better
than mere emotion. Fully to exhibit the grounds
of this claim of Christ upon us would involve an
examination of the Gospel narratives in detail : it
would involve an attempt to present to you what was
this teaching, this character, this religious consciousness which has commanded the homage of mankind.
To attempt such a task would be out of place in a
brief course of lectures devoted to a particular
aspect of Religion—its relation to Philosophy.
Here I must assume that you feel the spiritual
supremacy of Christ—his unique position in the
religious history of the world and his unique importance for the spiritual life of each one of us—; and go
on to ask what assertions such a conviction warrants
us in making about his person and nature, what in
short should be our attitude towards the traditional
doctrines of the Christian Church.

You may know something of the position taken
up in this matter by the dominant school of what
I may call believing liberal Theology in Germany—

the school which takes its name from the great
theologian Ritschl, but which will be best known to
most Englishmen in connexion with the name of Prof.
Harnack, though it may be well to remember that
Harnack is nearer to the' left than to the right wing
of that school. The fundamental principle of that
school is to base the claims of Christianity mainly
úpon the appeal which the picture of the life, teaching,
character, and personality of Christ makes to the
moral and religious consciousness of mankind. Their
teaching is Christo-centric in the highest possible
degree : but they are almost or entirely indifferent
to the dogmatic formulæ which may be employed to
express this supreme religious importance of Christ.
In putting the personal and historical Christ, and
not any doctrine about him, in the centre of the
religious life I believe they are right. But this
principle is sometimes asserted in an exaggerated
and one-sided manner. In the first place they are
somewhat contemptuous of Philosophy, and of philosophic argument even for such fundamental truths
as the existence of God. I do not see that the
subjective impression made by Christ can by itself
prove the fact of God's existence. We must first
believe that there is a God to be revealed before
we can be led to believe in Christ as the supreme
Revealer. I do not believe that the modern world
will permanently accept a view of the Universe

which does not commend itself to its Reason. The
Ritschlians talk about the truth of Religion resting
upon value-judgements. I can quite understand that
a value-judgement may tell us the supreme value of
Christ's character and his fitness to be treated as the
representative of God to us, when once we believe
in God : but I cannot see how any value-judgement
taken by itself can assure us of that existence.
Value is one thing : existence is another. To my
mind a Christian Apologetic should begin, like the
old Apologies of Justin or Aristides, with showing
the essential reasonableness of Christ's teaching
about God and its essential harmony with the
highest philosophic teaching about duty, about the
divine nature, about the soul and its eternal destiny.
The Ritschlian is too much disposed to underrate
the value of all previous religious and ethical teaching, even of Judaism at its highest : he is not content
with making Christ the supreme Revealer : he wants
to make him the only Revealer. And when we turn
to post-Christian religious history, he is apt to treat
all the great developments of religious and ethical
thought from the time of the Apostles to our own
day as simply worthless and even mischievous
corruptions of the original, and only genuine, Christianity. He tends to reduce Christianity to the
ipsissima verba of its Founder. The Ritschlian
dislikes Dogma, not because it may be at times a

misdevelopment, but because it is a development ;
not because some of it may be antiquated Philosophy,
but simply because it is Philosophy.[1]

In order to treat fairly this question of doctrinal
development, it must be remembered that what is
commonly called dogma is only a part—perhaps
not the most important part—of that development.
Supreme as I believe to be the value of Christ's
great principle of Brotherhood, it is impossible to
deny that, if we look in detail at the moral ideal
of any educated Christian at the present day, we
shall find in it many elements which cannot explicitly
be discovered in the *ipsissima verba* of Christ and
still less of his Apostles. And development in the
ethical ideal always carries with it some development
in a man's conception of God and the Universe.
Some of these elements are due to a gradual bringing
out into clear consciousness, and an application to
new details, of principles latent in the actual words
of Christ ; others to an infusion of Greek Philosophy ;
others to the practical experience and the scientific
discoveries of the modern world. Christianity in
the course of nineteen centuries has gradually
absorbed into itself many ideas from various sources,

----

[1] In their assertion of the necessity of Development, and of the
religious community as the origin of Development, the teaching of
the Abbé Loisy and the Roman Catholic Modernists seems to me to
be complementary to that of the Ritschlians, though I do not always
accept their rather destructive critical conclusions.

christianizing them in the process. Many ideas,
much Hellenic Philosophy, many Hellenic ideals of
life, many Roman ideas of government and organiza-
tion have thus, in the excellent phrase of Professor
Gardner, been ' baptized into Christ.' This capacity
of absorbing into itself elements of spiritual life
which were originally independent of it is not a
defect of historical Christianity, but one of its
qualifications for being accepted by the modern
world as a universal, an absolute, a final Religion.

It does not seem to me possible to recognize the
claim of any historical Religion to be final and
ultimate, unless it include within itself a principle
of development. Let me, as briefly as I can, illustrate what I mean. It is most clearly and easily
seen in the case of Morality. If the idea of a
universal Religion is to mean that any detailed
code of Morals laid down at a definite moment of
history can serve by itself for the guidance of all
human life in all after ages, we may at once dismiss
the notion as a dream. In nothing did our Lord
show his greatness and the fitness of his Religion
for universality more than in abstaining from
drawing up such a code. He confined himself
to laying down a few great principles, with
illustrations applicable to the circumstances of
his immediate hearers. Those principles require
development and application to the needs and

circumstances of successive ages before they can
suffice to guide us in the details of conduct. To
effect this development and application has been
historically the work of the Church which owes its
origin to the disciples whom he gathered around
him. If we may accept the teaching of the fourth
Gospel as at least having germs in the actual
utterances of our Lord, he himself foresaw the
necessity of such a development. At all events
the belief in the continued work of God's Spirit
in human Society is an essential principle of the
Christian Religion as it was · taught by the first
followers of its Founder. Take for instance the case
of slavery. Our Lord never condemned slavery :
it is not certain that he would have done so,
had the case been presented to him. Very likely
his answer would have been 'Who made me a judge
or a divider,' or 'Render unto Cæsar the things that
are Cæsar's.' No one on reflection can now fail to
see the essential incompatibility between slavery
and the Christian spirit ; yet it was perhaps fourteen
hundred years before a single Christian thinker
definitely enunciated that incompatibility, and more
than eighteen hundred years before slavery was
actually banished from all nominally Christian
lands. Who can doubt that many features of our
existing social system are equally incompatible with
the principles of Christ's teaching, and that the

accepted Christian morality of a hundred years
hence will definitely condemn many things which
the average Christian Conscience now allows ?

And then there is another kind of development
in Ethics which is equally necessary. The Christian
law of Love bids us promote the true good of our
fellow-men, bids us regard another man's good as
equally valuable with our own or with the like good
of any other. But what is this good life which we
are to promote ? As to that our Lord has only
laid down a few very general principles—the supreme
value of Love itself, the superiority of the spiritual
to the carnal, the importance of sexual purity.
These principles our consciences still acknowledge,
and there are no others of equal importance. But
what of the intellectual life ? Has that no value ?
Our Lord never depreciated it, as so many religious
founders and reformers have done. But he has
given us no explicit guidance about it. When the
Christian ideal embraced within itself a recognition
of the value and duty of Culture, it was borrowing
from Greece. And when we turn from Ethics to
Theology, the actual fact of development is no less
indisputable. Every alteration of the ethical ideal
has brought with it some alteration in our idea of
God. We can no longer endure theories of the
Atonement which are opposed to modern ideas of
Justice, though they were quite compatible with

patristic or medieval ideas of Justice. The advances
of Science have altered our whole conception of God's
mode of acting upon or governing the world. None
of these things are religiously so important as the
great principle of the Fatherhood of God, nor have
they in any way tended to modify its truth or its
supreme importance. But they do imply that our
Theology is not and cannot be in all points the same
as that of the first Christians.

Now with these presuppositions let us approach
the question of that great structure of formal dogma
which the Church has built upon the foundation
of Christ's teaching. A development undoubtedly
it is ; but, while we must not assume that every
development which has historically taken place is
necessarily true or valuable, it is equally unphilo-
sophical to assume that, because it is a development,
it is necessarily false or worthless. Our Lord himself
did, indeed, claim to be the Messiah ; the fact of
Messiahship was what was primarily meant by the
title ' Son of God.' Even in the Synoptists he exhibits
a consciousness of a direct divine mission supremely
important for his own race ; and, before the close, we
can perhaps discover a growing conviction that the
truth which he was teaching was meant for a larger
world. Starting from and developing these ideas, his
followers set themselves to devise terms which should
express their own sense of their Master's unique

religious value and importance, to express what
they felt he had been to their own souls, what
they felt he might be to all who accepted his
message.   Even to St. Paul the term 'Son of God'
still meant primarily 'the Messiah': but in the
light of his conception of Jesus, the Messianic idea
expanded till the Christ was exalted to a position
far above anything which Jewish prophecy or
Apocalypse had ever claimed for him.   And the
means of expressing these new ideas were found
naturally and inevitably in the current philosophical
terminology of the day.   With the fourth Gospel,
if not already with St. Paul, there was infused into
the teaching of the Church a new element.   From
the Jewish-Alexandrian speculative Theology the
author borrowed the term Logos to express what he
conceived to be the cosmic importance of Christ's
position.   He accepted from that speculation—probably from Philo—the theory which personified or
half-personified that Logos or Wisdom of God
through which God was represented in the Old
Testament as creating the world and inspiring the
prophets.   This Logos through whom God had
throughout the ages been more and more fully
revealing Himself had at last become actually
incarnate in Jesus Christ.   This Word of God is
also described as truly God, though in the fourth
Gospel the relation of the Father to the Word—at

least to the Word before the Incarnation—is left
wholly vague and undefined.

From these comparatively simple beginnings
sprang centuries of controversy culminating in that
elaborate system of dogma which is often little
understood even by its most vigorous champions.
You know in a very general way the result. The
Logos was made more and more distinct from God,
endowed with a more and more decidedly personal
existence. Then, when the interests of Monotheism
seemed to be endangered, the attempt was made to
save it by asserting the subordination of the Son to
the Father. The result was that by Arianism the
Son was reduced to the position of an inferior God.
Polytheism had once more to be averted by asserting in even stronger terms not merely the equality
of the Son with the Father but also the Unity of the
God who is both Father and Son. The doctrine of
the Divinity of the Holy Ghost went through a somewhat similar series of stages. At first regarded as
identical with the Word, a distinction was gradually
effected. The Word was said to have been incarnate
in Jesus; while it was through the Holy Ghost that
the subsequent work of God was carried on in human
hearts. And by similar stages the equality of the
Holy Ghost to Father and to Son was gradual y
evolved; while it was more and more strongly
asserted that, in spite of the eternal distinction of

Persons, it was one and the same God who revealed
Himself in all the activities attributed to each of
them.

Side by side with these controversies about the
relation between the Father and the Word, there
was a gradual development of doctrine as to the
relation between the Logos and the human Jesus
in whom he took up his abode. Frequently the idea
of any real humanity in Jesus was all but lost. That
was at last saved by the Catholic formula 'perfect God and perfect man'; though it cannot be
denied that popular thought in all ages has never
quite discarded the tendency to think of Jesus as
simply God in human form, and not really man at
all. Even now there are probably hundreds of people
who regard themselves as particularly orthodox
Churchmen who yet do not know that the Church
teaches that our Lord had a human soul and a
human will.

What are we to make of all that vast structure,
of the elaboration and complication of which the
Constantinopolitan Creed which we miscall Nicene
and even the so-called Athanasian Creed give very
little idea to those who do not also know something
of the Councils, the Fathers, and the Schoolmen ?
Has it all a modern meaning ? Can it be translated
into terms of our modern thought and speech ? For
I suppose it hardly needs demonstration—that such

translation is necessary, if it be possible. I doubt whether any man in this audience who has not made a special study of the subject, will get up and say that the meaning of such terms as 'substance,' 'essence,' 'nature,' 'hypostasis,' 'person,' 'eternal generation,' 'procession,' 'hypostatic union,' and the like is at once evident to him by the light of nature and an ordinary modern education. And those who know most about the matter will most fully realize the difficulty of saying exactly what was meant by such phrases at this or that particular moment or by this or that particular thinker. A thorough discussion of this subject from the point of view of one who acknowledges the supreme claims of Christ upon the modern mind, and is yet willing fairly to examine the traditional Creed in the light of modern philosophical culture, is a task which very much needs to be undertaken. I doubt if it has been satisfactorily performed yet. Even if I possessed a tithe of the learning necessary for that task, I could obviously not undertake it now. But a few remarks on the subject may be of use for the guidance of our personal religious life in this matter:

(1) I should like once more to emphasize the fact that the really important thing, from the point of view of the spiritual life of the individual soul, is our personal attitude towards our Lord himself and his teaching, and not the phrases in which we express

it. A man who believes what Christ taught about
God's Fatherhood, about human brotherhood and
human duty, about sin, the need for repentance,
the Father's readiness to forgive, the value of Prayer,
the certainty of Immortality—the man who finds
the ideal of his life in the character of Jesus, and
strives by the help which he has supplied to think
of God and feel towards God as he did, to imitate
him in his life, to live (like him) in communion with
the Father and in the hope of Immortality—he is a
Christian, and a Christian in the fullest sense of the
word. He will find in that faith all that is necessary
(to use the old phrase) for salvation—for personal
goodness and personal Religion. And such a man
will be saved, and saved through Christ; even though
he has never heard of the Creeds, or deliberately
rejects many of the formulæ which the Church or
the Churches have 'built upon' that one foundation.

(2) At the same time, if we believe in the supreme
importance of Christ for the world, for the religious
life of the Church and of the individual, it is surely
convenient to have some language in which to express
our sense of that importance. The actual personal
attitude towards Christ is the essential thing: but
as a means towards that attitude it is of importance
to express what Christ has actually been to others,
and what he ought to be to ourselves. Children

and adults alike require to have the claims of Christ
presented to them before they can verify them by
their own experience : and this requires articulate
language of some kind. Religion can only be
handed down, diffused, propagated by an organized
society : and a religious society must have some
means of handing on its religious ideas. It is possible
to hold that under other conditions a different set
of terms might have expressed the truth as well as
those which have actually been enshrined in the
New Testament, the Liturgies, and the Creeds. But
the phrases which have been actually adopted surely
have a strong presumption in their favour, even if
it were merely through the difficulty of changing
them, and the importance of unity, continuity,
corporate life. It is easier to explain, or even if
need be, alter in some measure the meaning of an
accepted formula than to introduce a new one.
Religious development has at all times taken place
largely in this way. Our Lord himself entirely
transformed the meaning of God's Fatherhood,
Messiahship, the Kingdom of God, the people of
God, the true Israel. At all events we should
endeavour to discover the maximum of truth that
any traditional formula can be made to yield before
we discard it in favour of a new one. If we want
to worship and to work with Christ's Church, we
must do our best to give the maximum of meaning

to the language in which it expresses its faith and
its devotion.

(3) We must insist strongly upon the thoroughly
human character of Christ's own consciousness.
Jesus did not—so I believe the critical study of the
Gospels leads us to think—himself claim to be God,
or to be Son of God in any sense but that of
Messiahship. He claimed to speak with authority :
he claimed a divine mission : he claimed to be a Revealer of divine truth. The fourth Gospel has been
of infinite service to spiritual Christianity. It has
given the world a due sense of the spiritual importance of Christ as the Way, the Truth, and the Life.
Perhaps Christianity could hardly have expanded
into a universal Religion without that Gospel. But
we cannot regard all that the Johannine Christ says
about himself as the *ipsissima verba* of Jesus. The
picture is idealized in accordance with the writer's
own conceptions, though after all its Theology is
very much simpler than the later Theology which
has grown out of it permits most people to see. We
must not let these discourses blind us to the human
character of Christ's consciousness. And this real
humanity must carry with it the recognition of the
thoroughly human limitations of his knowledge.
The Bishop of Birmingham has prepared the way
for the union of a really historical view of Christ's
life with a reasonable interpretation of the Catholic

doctrine about him, by reviving the ancient view as
to the limitation of his intellectual knowledge;[1] but
the principle must be carried in some ways further
than the Bishop himself would be prepared to go.
The accepted Christology must be distinctly recognized as the Church's reflection and comment upon
Christ's work and its value, not as the actual teaching
of the Master about himself.

(4) It must likewise be recognized that the language
in which the Church expressed this attitude towards
Christ was borrowed from Greek Metaphysics, particularly from Plato and Neo-Platonism in the
patristic period, and from Aristotle in the Middle
Ages.   And we cannot completely separate language
from thought.   It was not merely Greek technical
phrases but Greek ways of thinking which were
imported into Catholic Christianity.   And the language, the categories, the ideas of Greek Philosophy
were to some extent different from those of modern
times.   The most Platonically-minded thinker of
modern times does not really think exactly as Plato
thought : the most Catholic-minded thinker of
modern times, if he has also breathed the atmosphere
of modern Science and modern Culture, cannot really
think exactly as Athanasius or Basil thought.   I

[1] In his Essay in *Lux Mundi* (1889).   He has since developed his
view in his Bampton Lectures on *The Incarnation of the Son of
God* and a volume of *Dissertations on Subjects connected with the
Incarnation.*

do not suppose that any modern mind can think itself back into exactly the state of mind which an ancient Father was in, when he used the term Logos. This central idea of the Logos is not a category of modern thought. We cannot really think of a Being who is as distinct from the Father as he is represented as being in some of the patristic utterances—I say advisedly some, for widely different modes of thought are found in Fathers of equal authority—and yet so far one with him that we can say 'One God, one spiritual Being, and not two.' Nor are we under any obligation to accept these formulæ as representing profound mysteries which we cannot understand : they were simply pieces of metaphysical thinking, some of them valuable and successful pieces of thinking, others less so. We must use them as helps, not as fetters to our thought. But, though we cannot think ourselves back into exactly the same intellectual condition as a fourth- or fifth-century Father, there is no reason why we should not recognize the fundamental truth of the religious idea which he was trying to express. A modern Philosopher would probably express that thought somewhat in this manner. 'The whole world is a revelation of God in a sense, and still more so is the human mind : all through the ages God has gone on revealing Himself more and more in human consciousness, especially through the prophets and other exceptionally inspired men. The fullest and completest revelation of Himself was made once for all in the person and teaching of Jesus, in whom we recognize a revelation of God adequate to all our spiritual needs, when developed and interpreted by the continued presence of God's Spirit in the world and particularly in the Church which grew out of the little company of Jesus' friends.'

(5) I do not think at the present day even quite orthodox people are much concerned about the technicalities of the conciliar Theology, or even about the niceties of the Athanasian Creed. They are even a little suspicious sometimes that much talk about the doctrine of the Logos is only intended to evade a plain answer to the supreme question of the Divinity of Christ. You will expect me perhaps to say something about that question. I would first observe that the popular term ' divinity of Christ' is apt to give a somewhat misleading impression of what the orthodox teaching on the subject really is. For one thing, it is apt to suggest the idea of a pre-existent human consciousness of Jesus, which would be contrary to Catholic teaching. The Logos—the eternal Son or Reason of God—pre-existed; but not the man Jesus Christ who was born at a particular moment of history, and who is still, according to Catholic Theology, a distinct human soul perfectly and for ever united with the Word.

And then again, it is apt to suggest the heretical idea that the whole Trinity was incarnate in Christ, and not merely the Word.   Orthodox Theology does not teach that God the Father became incarnate in Christ, and suffered upon the Cross.   And lastly, the constant iteration of the phrase 'Divinity of Christ' tends to the concealment of the other half of the Catholic doctrine—the real humanity of Christ. To speak of the God-manhood of Christ or the in-dwelling of God in Christ would be a truer representa-tion even of the strictest orthodox doctrine, apart from all modern re-interpretations.   But even so, when all this is borne in mind, it may be asked, What is the real meaning of saying that a man was also God ?   I would answer, 'Whether it is possible to give a modern, intelligible, philosophically defensible meaning to the idea of Christ's Divinity depends entirely upon the question what we conceive to be the true relation between Humanity in general and God.'   If (as I have attempted to show) we are justified in thinking of all human consciousness as constituting a partial reproduction of the divine Mind ; if we are justified in thinking of human Reason, and particularly of the human Conscience, as constituting in some measure and in some sense a revelation by means of which we can rise to a contemplation of the divine nature ; if Personality (as we know it in man) is the highest category within our knowledge ; then there is a real meaning in talking of one particular man being also divine; of the divine Reason or Logos as dwelling after a unique, exceptional, pre-eminent manner in him.

As Dr. Edward Caird has remarked, all the metaphysical questions which were formerly discussed as to the relation between the divine and the human nature in Christ, are now being discussed again in reference to the relation of Humanity in general to God. We cannot say intelligibly that God dwells in Christ, unless we have already recognized that in a sense God dwells and reveals Himself in Humanity at large, and in each particular human soul. But I fully recognize that, if this is all that is meant by the expression 'divinity of Christ,' that doctrine would be evacuated of nearly all that makes it precious to the hearts of Christian people. And therefore it is all-important that we should go on to insist that men do not reveal God equally. The more developed intellect reveals God more completely than that of the child or the savage: and (far more important from a religious point of view), the higher and more developed moral consciousness reveals Him more than the lower, and above all the actually better man reveals God more than the worse man. Now, if in the life, teaching, and character of Christ—in his moral and religious consciousness, and in the life and character which

so completely expressed and illustrated that consciousness—we can discover the highest revelation
of the divine nature, we can surely attach a real
meaning to the language of the Creeds which
singles him out from all the men that ever lived
as the one in whom the ideal relation of man to
God is most completely realized. If God can only
be known as revealed in Humanity, and Christ
is the highest representative of Humanity, we can
very significantly say 'Christ is *the* Son of God,
very God of very God, of one substance with the
Father,' though the phrase undoubtedly belongs
to a philosophical dialect which we do not habitually use.

(6) Behind the doctrine of the Incarnation looms
the still more technical doctrine of the Trinity. Yet
after all, it is chiefly, I believe, as a sort of necessary
background or presupposition to the idea of Christ's
divine nature that modern religious people, not
professionally interested in Theology, attach importance to that doctrine. They accept the doctrine
in so far as it is implied by the teaching of Scripture
and by the doctrine of our Lord's Divinity, but they
are not much attached to the technicalities of the
Athanasian Creed. The great objection to that
Creed, apart from the damnatory clauses, is the
certainty that it will be misunderstood by most of
those who think they understand it at all. The

best thing we could do with the Athanasian Creed is
to drop it altogether : the next best thing to it is
to explain it, or at least so much of it as really
interests the ordinary layman—the doctrine of three
Persons in one God. And therefore it is important
to insist in the strongest possible way that the
word ' Person ' which has most unfortunately come
to be the technical term for what the Greeks more
obscurely called the three ὑποστάσεις in the Godhead
does not, and never did, mean what we commonly
understand by Personality—whether in the language
of ordinary life or of modern Philosophy. I do not
deny that at certain periods Theology did tend to
think of the Logos as a distinct being from the
Father, a distinct consciousness with thoughts, will,
desires, emotions not identical with those of God
the Father. The distinction was at times pushed
to a point which meant either sheer Tritheism, or
something which is incapable of being distinctly
realized in thought at all. But that is scarcely true
of the Theology which was finally accepted either
by East or West. This is most distinctly seen in
the *Summa Theologica* of St. Thomas Aquinas : and I
would remind you that you cannot be more orthodox
than St. Thomas—the source not only of the Theology
professed by the Pope and taught in every Roman
Seminary but of the Theology embodied in our own
Articles. St. Thomas' explanation of the Trinity

is that God is at one and the same time Power or
Cause[1] (Father), Wisdom (Sòn), Will (Holy Ghost); or,
since the Will of God is always a loving Will, Love
(Amor) is sometimes substituted for Will (Voluntas)
in explanation of the Holy Spirit.[2] How little St.

[1] I venture thus to translate 'Principium' (ἀρχή); in Abelard and
his disciple Peter the Lombard, the famous Master of the Sentences,
the word is 'Potentia' (L. I. Dist. xxxiv.): and St. Thomas himself
(P. I. Q. xli. Art. 4) explains 'Principium' by 'Potentia generandi
Filium.'

[2] Thus in *Summa Theologica*, Pars I. Q. xxxvii. Art. 1, the
'conclusio' is 'Amor, peisonaliter acceptus, proprium nomen est
Spiritus sancti,' which is explained to mean that there are in the Godhead 'duæ processiones: una per modum intellectus, quæ est processio
Verbi; alia per modum voluntatis, quæ est processio amoris.' So
again (*ibid.* Q. xlv. Art. 7): 'In creaturis igitur rationalibus, in
quibus est intellectus et voluntas, invenitur repræsentatio Trinitatis
per modum imaginis, inquantum invenitur in eis Verbum con-
ceptum, et amor procedens.' In a friendly review of my Essay in
Contentio Veritatis, in which I endeavoured to expound in a modern
form this doctrine, Dr. Sanday (*Journal of Theological Studies*, vol.
iv., 1903) wrote: 'One of the passages that seem to me most open to
criticism is that on the doctrine of the Trinity (p. 48). "Power,
Wisdom, and Will" surely cannot be a sound trichotomy as applied
either to human nature or Divine. Surely Power is an expression of
Will and not co-ordinate with it. The common division, Power (or
Will), Wisdom, and Love is more to the point. Yet Dr. Rashdall
identifies the two triads by what I must needs think a looseness of
reasoning.' The Margaret Professor of Divinity hardly seems to
recognize that he is criticizing the Angelical Doctor and not myself. If
Dr. Sanday had had the formulation of the doctrine of the Trinity,
the result, if less metaphysically subtle, might no doubt have proved
more easily intelligible to the modern mind; but the 'identification' of which he complains happens to be part of the traditional
doctrine, and I was endeavouring merely to make the best of it for
modern Christians. I add St. Thomas' justification of it, which is
substantially what I gave in *Contentio Veritatis* and have repeated
above: 'Cum processiones divinas secundum aliquas actiones
necesse est accipere, secundum bonitatem, et hujusmodi alia attributa,
non accipiuntur aliæ processiones, nisi Verbi et amoris, secundum

Thomas thought of the 'Persons' as separate consciousnesses, is best seen from his doctrine (taken
from Augustine) that the love of the Father for the Son
is the Holy Spirit. The love of one Being for himself
or for another is not a Person in the natural, normal,
modern sense of the word : and it would be quite
unorthodox to attribute Personality to the Son in
any other sense than that in which it is attributed
to the Holy Ghost.   I do not myself attach any great
importance to these technical phrases.   I do not

quod Deus suam essentiam, veritatem et bonitatem intelligit et
amat' (Q. xxvii. Art. 5).   The source of the doctrine is to be found in
St. Augustine, who habitually speaks of the Holy Spirit as Amor; but,
when he refers to the 'Imago Trinitatis' in man the Spirit is
represented sometimes by 'Amor,' sometimes by 'Voluntas' (*de Trin.*,
L. xiv. cap 7).   The other two members of the human triad are
with him 'Memoria' (or 'Mens') and 'Intelligentia.'

With regard to the difficulty of distinguishing Power from Will, I was
perhaps to blame for not giving St. Thomas' own word 'Principium.'
The word ' Principium' means the πηγὴ θεότητος, the ultimate Cause
or Source of Being : by 'Voluntas' St. Thomas means that actual
putting forth of Power (in knowing and in loving the Word or Thought
eternally begotten by God the Father) which is the Holy Ghost.   I
am far from saying that the details of St. Thomas' doctrine are not
open to much criticism : a rough correspondence between his teaching
and any view of God's Nature which can commend itself to a modern
Philosopher is all that I endeavoured to point out.   The modern
thinker would no doubt with Dr. Sanday prefer the triad 'Power,
Wisdom, Love,' or (I would suggest) 'Feeling, including Love as the
highest form of Feeling.'   The reason why St. Thomas will not accept
such an interpretation is that his Aristotelianism (here not very con-
sonant with the Jewish and Christian view of God) excludes all feeling
or emotion from the divine nature : ' Love' has therefore to be identified with ' Will ' and not with 'Feeling.' I cannot but think that the
Professor might have taken a little more trouble to understand both
St. Thomas and myself before accusing either of us of 'looseness
of reasoning.'

deny that the supremely important truth that God
has received His fullest revelation in the historical
Christ, and that He goes on revealing Himself in the
hearts of men, might have been otherwise, more
simply, to modern minds more intelligibly, expressed.
There are detailed features of the patristic or the
scholastic version of the doctrine which involve
conceptions to which the most accomplished Professors of Theology would find it difficult or impossible to give a modern meaning.   I do not know
for instance that much would have been lost had
Theology (with the all but canonical writers Clement
of Rome and Hermas, with Ignatius, with Justin,
with the philosophic Clement of Alexandria) continued to speak indifferently of the Word and the
Spirit.   Yet taken by itself this Thomist doctrine
of the Trinity is one to which it is quite possible to
give a perfectly rational meaning, and a meaning
probably very much nearer to that which was really
intended by its author than the meaning which is
usually put upon the Trinitarian formula by popular
religious thought.   That God is Power, and Wisdom,
and Love is simply the essence of Christian Theism—
not the less true because few Unitarians would
repudiate it.

(7) Once more let me briefly remind you that any
claim for finality in the Christian Religion must be
based on its power of perpetual development.

Belief in the continued work of the Holy Spirit in
the Church is an essential element of the Catholic
Faith. We need not, with the Ritschlian, con-
temptuously condemn the whole structure of
Christian doctrine because undoubtedly it is a
development of what was taught by Christ himself.
Only, if we are to justify the development of the past,
we must go on to assert the same right and duty of
development in Ethics and in Theology for the
Church of the future. In the pregnant phrase of
Loisy, the development which the Church is most
in need of at the present moment is precisely a
development in the idea of development itself.

But how can we tell (it may be asked), if we once
admit that the development of Religion does not
end with the teaching of Christ, where the development will stop ? If we are to admit an indefinite
possibility of growth and change, how do we know
that Christianity itself will not one day be outgrown ?
If we once admit that the final appeal is to the
religious consciousness of the present, we must
acknowledge that it is not possible to demonstrate
a *priori* that the Christian Religion is the final,
universal, or absolute Religion. All we can say is
that we have no difficulty in recognizing that the
development which has so far taken place, in so far
as it is a development which we can approve and
accept, seems to us a development which leaves the

Religion still essentially the Religion of Christ. In
the whole structure of the modern Christian's religious
belief, that which was contributed by Christ himself
is incomparably the most important part—the basis
of the whole structure. The essentials of Religion
and Morality still seem to us to be contained in his
teaching as they are contained nowhere else. All
the rest that is included in an enlightened modern
Christian's religious creed is either a direct working
out of the principles already contained there, or (if
it has come from other sources) it has been transformed in the process of adaptation. Nothing has
been discovered in Religion and Morality which
tends in any way to diminish the unique reverence
which we feel for the person of Christ, the perfect
sufficiency of his character to represent and incarnate
for us the character of God. It is a completely
gratuitous assumption to suppose that it will ever
lose that sufficiency. Even in the development of
Science, there comes a time when its fundamentals
are virtually beyond the reach of reconsideration.
Still more in practical life, mere unmotived, gratuitous
possibilities may be disregarded. It weakens the
hold of fundamental convictions upon the mind to
be perpetually contemplating the possibility or
probability of fundamental revision. We ought no
doubt to keep the spiritual ear ever open that we
may always be hearing what the Spirit saith unto

the Churches. But to look forward to a time when any better way will be discovered of thinking of God than Jesus' way of thinking of Him as a loving Father is as gratuitous as to contemplate the probability of something in human life at present unknown being discovered of greater value than Love. Until that discovery is made, our Religion will still remain the Religion of him who, by what he said and by what he was, taught the world to think of God as the supreme Love and the supreme Holiness, the source of all other love and all other holiness.

LITERATURE

The literature is here too vast to mention even the works of the very first importance : I can only select a very few books which have been useful to myself. The late Sir John Seeley's *Ecce Homo* may be regarded as in the light of modern research a somewhat uncritical book, but it remains to my mind the most striking expression of the appeal which Christ makes to the Conscience of the modern world. It has proved a veritable fifth Gospel to many seekers after light. Bishop Moorhouse's little book, *The Teaching of Christ,* will serve as an introduction to the study of Christ's life and work. A more elaborate treatment of the subject, with which I am very much in sympathy, is Wendt's *Teaching of Jesus.* The ideal life of Christ perhaps remains to be written. Professor Sanday's Article on ' Jesus Christ ' in Hastings' *Dictionary of the Bible* may be mentioned as a good representative of moderate and scholarly Conservatism or Liberal Conservatism. Professor Oscar Holtzmann's *Life of Jesus* is based on more radical, perhaps over-radical, criticism. Professor Harnack's

What is Christianity? has become the typical expression of
the Ritschlian attitude. The ideas of extreme Roman Catholic
'Modernism' may be gathered from Loisy's *l'Évangile et
l'Église* and *Autour d'un Petit Livre*. Professor Gardner's
three books—*Exploratio Evangelica*, the shorter *An Historic
View of the New Testament*, and *The Growth of Christianity*
—may be especially commended to those who wish to satisfy
themselves that a thorough-going recognition of the results
of historical Criticism is compatible with a whole-hearted
personal acceptance of Christianity. Dr. Fairbairn's *Philosophy of the Christian Religion* and Bousset's *What is Religion?*
are especially valuable as vindications of the supreme position
of Christianity combined with the fullest recognition of the
measure of Revelation contained in all the great historical
Religions. Allen's *Continuity of Christian Thought* suggests
what seems to me the right attitude of the modern thinker
towards traditional dogma, though the author's position is
more decidedly 'Hegelian' than mine. I may also mention
Professor Inge's contribution to *Contentio Veritatis* on 'The
Personal Christ,' and some of the Essays in *Lux Hominum*.
Though I cannot always agree with him, I recognize the high
value of the Bishop of Birmingham's Bampton Lectures on
The Divinity of Jesus Christ the Son of God and the accom-
panying volume of *Dissertations*.